HINDUISM

Religion

Editor

THE REV. PROFESSOR E. O. JAMES
MA, D.LITT, PH.D, DD, FSA

formerly Professor of the History and Philosophy of Religion
in the University of London

HINDUISM

A. C. Bouquet
formerly Lecturer in the History and Comparative Study of Religion
in the University of Cambridge

HUTCHINSON UNIVERSITY LIBRARY
LONDON

HUTCHINSON & CO (*Publishers*) LTD
178–202 Great Portland Street, London W1

London Melbourne Sydney
Auckland Bombay Toronto
Johannesburg New York

First published 1949
Second (revised) edition 1962
Reprinted 1966, 1969

*The picture on the cover of the paperback edition
shows Siva, in his form as Natarajan, performing the dance of life. It is reproduced by courtesy
of the Victoria and Albert Museum, Crown
copyright.*

*This book has been set in Bembo, printed in Great Britain
on Smooth Wove paper by Anchor Press, and
bound by Wm. Brendon, both of Tiptree, Essex*

09 030671 6 (cased)

09 030672 4 (paper)

To the memory of
Charles Freer Andrews

CONTENTS

Acknowledgments   9

Preface   11

Introduction   13

1 Early beginnings   19

2 The religion of the Vedic age   26

3 The age of the Upanishads   43

4 The great movements. Jainism and Buddhism   62

5 The change to incarnational religion. The great epics. The
   Bhagavadgita. The beginnings of Bhakti   73

6 Hinduism during the medieval period. Sankara, Ramanuja,
   and the growth of Bhakti   84

7 Islam in India and its consequences. Later Bhakti. Saktism   97

8 The British occupation and its effects; reforming movements
   and personalities   109

9 Religious observances: Hinduism as a working system   122

10 Self-government and the future of Hinduism   142

Note to 1962 edition   148

Index   153

ACKNOWLEDGMENTS

My special thanks are due to the following: to Meridian Books, Ltd, for permission to quote from Pandit Nehru's book, *The Discovery of India*; to the Clarendon Press, Oxford, for permission to quote from Dr G. U. Pope's translation of the Tiruvasagam; to Messrs John Murray for permission to quote from Dr E. J. Thomas's translation of the Bhagavadgita ('The Song of the Lord') in the series *The Wisdom of the East*, and also from his translations of Vedic Hymns in the same series; to Messrs Edward Arnold & Co for permission to quote from Sir Charles Eliot's *Hinduism and Buddhism*; to the YMCA Publishing House, Calcutta, for permission to quote from Dr Nicol MacNicol's *Psalms of the Maratha Saints*; to the Oxford University Press for permission to quote from Dr R. E. Hume's work *The Thirteen Principal Upanishads* and from Mrs Stevenson's *The Rites of the Twice-Born*.

PREFACE

The object of this brief treatise is twofold.

First, to present an introductory outline of the story of Hinduism from the earliest times to the present day, and to pave the way for further and more detailed study as well as to interest the general reader.

Second, to exhibit Hinduism as an *event* rather than as something static; as an organism, developing, reforming itself, and even changing and absorbing new elements, rather than as a rigid creed, or even as a survival from the past.

The reader should therefore find that the book has a sort of plot, which runs through from chapter to chapter, with Chapter 3 as the core of the work. This chapter, I fully recognise, is rather a long one, and perhaps more difficult than the others. But if the student will take trouble to master it, he will, I think, find the rest pretty plain sailing.

A European like myself can only expect to perform the task which has been allotted to him, as a mere spectator; and whatever advantages he may derive from detachment, they will be completely nullified, unless he also shows understanding and sympathy. I have done my best to exhibit both, and also, by submitting my work to Indian experts, to avoid any actual misstatements.

Perhaps it brings a slight gain to one's perspective that one is engaged in the work of studying a number of religions simultaneously. Certainly it makes easier the task of interpretation, and enables one from time to time to use an illustration for the purpose of bringing out the significance of some fact.

I wish to thank the following for their kind help, advice, and criticism: Pandit Jawaharlal Nehru, formerly of Trinity College; H.H. Prince Bhanj Deo of Magdalene College; Professor Dasgupta of Trinity College; Professor J. H. Hutton, Wyse Professor of Social Anthropology at Cambridge; The Rt. Reverend Stephen Neill, late Bishop of Tinnevelly; and Mr S. K. Mitra of the University of London. For the opinions expressed herein I alone am responsible. I have tried to make all other necessary acknowledgments in the footnotes and references, and to help the reader who wishes to pursue the subject further, by appending a short bibliography to each chapter.

My best thanks are due to Mr Hugh Montefiore, of St John's College, Oxford, for reading the proofs.

Cambridge, September 1948   A. C. BOUQUET

For the second edition I have written a few additional paragraphs which are printed on pages 148–51.

June 1962   A. C. BOUQUET

INTRODUCTION

A Frenchwoman quoted to me recently the saying of a distinguished modern Hindu,[1] to the effect that India's contribution to the treasures of the human race might be summed up as 'the efficiency of spirituality'. Whether the pages which follow will seem to the reader to confirm such a claim it is not for me to judge. My aim here is to give a detached and scientific account of a great human phenomenon, and to leave it at that.

*   *   *   *   *

The word Hindu is said not to be discoverable in ancient Indian literature. Indeed its first occurrence is reported in a work of the eighth century A.D., and there it means a *people*, and not an associate of a specific religion. Yet it is clear that it is a very old word, as it is found in the Zendavesta and in old Persian, and the peoples of Western and Central Asia used it to denote the inhabitants of an area beyond the River Indus. The early name for this river was Sindhu, and from the latter word 'Hindu' is obviously derived. A Chinese pilgrim, writing in the seventh century A.D., says that the central Asiatics called India 'Hindu' (he says Hsintu), but he continues, 'this is not at all a common name . . . and the most suitable title for it is "Aryadesha", which means "the Noble Land".'[2] The use of the word in connection with a particular religion is later still,[3] and probably comes in with the Moslem invasions (*see* Chapter 7). Hinduism then is the religion of

1 I think, Swami Vivekananda.
2 *The Discovery of India*, by Pandit Jawaharlal Nehru, p. 51.
3 Professor Dasgupta indeed thinks that this use of it may not date back more than three hundred years.

Hind or India, or at least of the greater part of its inhabitants. Hindustan is the Arab name for the whole country. The nearest Sanskrit
name for it is Bharata varsha. At the most recent census the population
amounted to approximately 400 millions, and of these about 66 per
cent are recorded as in some sense or other claiming to be Hindus.[4]

But in ancient times their forefathers did not themselves speak of
their religion as Hinduism, but as Arya Dharma, and it is significant
that the newest of all Indian temples, the Lakshmi-Narayan temple
at New Delhi, was built as recently as 1938 by a rich merchant, Seth
Raja Baldeolas Birla, 'for the benefit' (as is expressly stated) 'of the
different branches of Arya Dharma', and that it aims at including
under one roof not only orthodox Hindus, but Buddhists, Jains, Sikhs,
Arya-Samaj, Sanatanists or ultra-conservative Hindus, and even
Harijans or outcastes, as well as 'visitors from Europe and America
who are Aryans in origin, and are interested in Arya-Dharma'. The
enthusiasts of this new temple-foundation go so far as to say: 'The
spirit of Arya Dharma is . . . all comprehensive, and as such it embraces
even Christianity and Judaism, without meddling with their individual
differences.'

Nevertheless, in the Western world, Hinduism (and not Arya
Dharma) stands as the commonly used title of that specific religion,
which in the sub-continent is sharply distinguished from Islam. India
contains the largest single block of Moslems in the world. There are
more Moslems in it than in Arabia or Egypt. Yet India cannot as a
whole be described as a Moslem country, and although there are many
points in which Hindus and Moslems influence one another and even
borrow from each other, taken as a whole they are very different folk,
and though they may live near one another in the same village, they
stand apart in customs and general outlook.

Pandit Nehru has recently written:[5] 'Hinduism as a faith is vague,
amorphous, many-sided, all things to all men. It is hardly possible to
define it, or indeed to say precisely whether it is a religion or not, in
the usual sense of the word. In its present form, as well as in the past,
it embraces many beliefs and practices, from the highest to the lowest,

4 Dr. Betty Heimann gives the following figures as those of the Abstracts from the
census of India for 1941, which is the last available, and presumably the last which is
likely to be taken under British supervision:

Total population 388,997,955. Hindus 254,931,000, plus a further sixteen millions
among the primitive tribes; Moslems 92,058,000; Sikhs 5,691,447; Jains 1,449,286;
Buddhists 232,003; Christians 6,316,549, plus a further one million among the primitive
tribes; Parsis 114,890; Jews 22,480.

5 *The Discovery of India*, p. 52.

often opposed to or contradicting each other. Its essential spirit seems to be to live and let live.'

Although it is not correct to identify Hindu culture with Indian culture, it is true, nevertheless, that Hinduism, taken as a whole, is a culture quite as much as a religion. It is so much woven into the social structure of its adherents that the orthodox Hindu, like the Jew, if he should dare to give up his religion for any other, becomes by his choice an outcaste from his own people. It has recently been said that as long as one keeps out Christ, one can pack anything into Judaism.[6] The remark not only shows how curiously alike in many respects are the Hindu and Jewish communities (though in others extremely unlike), but it may also be parodied by saying: 'So long as one keeps out the idea that the historical process as such has any value for religion, one can pack anything into Hinduism.' Yet it is impossible for a foreigner to become a Hindu without at the same time being made a member of some caste or other, and by this means included in the structure of a national social order as well.

Within Hinduism, as within Catholicism, there is almost incredible variety. Heiler once declared that Catholicism included and tolerated at least seven distinct kinds of religion within a single institutional framework, and something of the same sort can be said of Hinduism. It is thus possible to find within its range philosophic mystics who disclaim belief in a personal Deity; fervent monotheists who direct their devotions towards a single personal God, of Whom and to Whom they speak in terms resembling those used by many Christians; and at the other extreme, crude animists whose main concern is with some local godling, generally a female tutelary divinity of the village, and polytheists of a type familiar to readers of Greek and Roman literature, closely resembling the scrupulously superstitious character outlined by Theophrastus.[7]

What makes Hinduism doubly hard to describe or even define is not only its vagueness, but also its variety, and its fluidity. It is not a static system, but a developing organism, full of movement. This fluidity it possesses in common with other great religions, but to a far greater degree. Parts of it no doubt appear extremely rigid and conservative; but if one takes long enough views, one can see many changes and adaptations to altered conditions, many instances of new ideas being absorbed, or of old customs being modified or abandoned.

Mahatma Gandhi tried, not very successfully, to give a definition of

6 A writer in the *International Review of Missions*.

7 Theophrastus: Characters: ὁ δεισιδαιμονεστερος (No. 16).

Hinduism in such terms as these: 'If I were asked, I should simply say: It is the search for truth through non-violent means. A man may not believe in God, and still call himself a Hindu. Hinduism is a relentless pursuit after truth. It is the religion of truth. Truth is God. Denial of God we have known. Denial of truth we have not known.' Pandit Nehru objects[8] to this that many Hindus do not accept non-violence as an essential part of Hindu belief, so that one is simply left with the equation, 'Hinduism is truth', or 'the search for truth', and this is really no definition at all, except perhaps of that common religious quest, which is not the peculiar property of Hindus, but may be said to distinguish all natural religion from that which claims to be revealed. Moreover orthodox Hinduism goes further than this, and claims a recorded revelation, embodied in the Vedas (q.v.).

There is undoubtedly a tendency on the part of modern Hindus to try to present their religion as capable of being detached from the peculiar limitations of caste, food-regulations, idol-worship, and even polytheism. They seem to be trying to make it undergo a transformation similar to that which the popular nationalist religion of Israel underwent during the period 750 B.C. to A.D. 100, and which eventually led to its partial transformation into that universalist religion which became known to the world as Christianity.

Thus in a recent pamphlet issued in Delhi we read: 'Arya Dharma is the common heritage of the entire human race. Its preservation and propagation are the sacred duty of every right-thinking and truth-loving man. . . . Social conditions and conventions have been given the status of religion by ignorant and foolish people . . . they cannot however be called religion. . . . Idol-worship, in a temple or elsewhere, is not an end in itself. It is simply a means to an end, that end being the concentration of the mind on God.' The writer goes on to invite the peoples of Europe and America to embrace Arya Dharma, and claims that its principles could be held by anyone who yet remained and called himself a Christian. 'Arya Dharma is the product of the pooling of all that is best in religious thought all over the world.'

There are critics who say that this competitive attempt to make Hinduism a universalist religion is provoked by the spectacle of Christian propaganda, and also by the very natural desire of a proud and ancient people not only to represent their religion as in no way inferior to that of other lands, but also to interpret it in such a manner as to make it *inclusive* of other religions. This may or may not be the case. In such a book as this one must express no opinion on the matter,

8 op. cit. p. 52.

but only record the fact of the attempt, and the criticism which it has provoked.

A great European indologist, Sir Charles Eliot, once wrote:[9] 'Hinduism has not been made, but has grown. It is a jungle, not a building. It is a living example of a great national paganism such as might have existed in Europe if Christianity had not become the state religion of the Roman Empire, if there had remained an incongruous jumble of old local superstitions, Greek philosophy, and oriental cults such as the worship of Sarapis or Mithras.' This seems true.

In India it is as though the whole non-Christian religious structure of the Mediterranean world of the first century A.D., including its philosophers, had been transferred bodily to an inaccessible country with a mainly tropical climate much nearer the Equator, left there for over a millennium, and then suddenly in the space of 150 years rediscovered a d confronted with a highly developed Christianity and an intensely progressive scientific civilisation. What we see today is the impact of these two latter forces upon a religious and social order which has for many centuries continued to exist in isolation from other areas on this planet, subject, of course, to the operation of the time-lag. Small wonder that on the one hand Dr. T. R. Glover, the classical scholar, felt when he visited India in 1915 that he was in a familiar atmosphere; and that, on the other hand, the religion of the Indian people should seem to Western visitors a confused amalgam of crass superstition and sublime world-negating mysticism, baffling yet arresting, and all the time yielding the impression that it might at any moment collapse into mere atheistic humanism.

How has it reached this condition, and what are its main distinctive features and its contributions to the spiritual life of the world? It will be my endeavour, in the pages which follow, to give some answer to each of these questions.

BOOKS FOR FURTHER STUDY

PANDIT JAWAHARLAL NEHRU. *The Discovery of India.* Meridian Press. 1946.

H. G. RAWLINSON. *India.* Cresset Press. 1937.

The Cambridge History of India. 6 vols. 1922.

SIR CHARLES ELIOT. *Hinduism and Buddhism.* Edw. Arnold. 3 vols. 1926.

The Legacy of India. Gen. editor, G. T. Garratt. Oxford. 1937.

9 Eliot. *Hinduism and Buddhism*, vol. i, p. 41.

B

I

EARLY BEGINNINGS

India is about half the size of the United States of America. Its total area is some 1,573,107 square miles,[1] and it contains nearly one-fifth of the human race, and at the time of writing, nearly three-quarters of the inhabitants of the British Commonwealth of Nations. In a space as large as Canada there are thirty-five times as many people, although they are concentrated in certain regions, while other parts, such as the great Indian desert in north-west Rajputana (which is hundreds of square miles in extent), are virtually uninhabited. Nearly one-quarter of the surface of British India is under forest.

A glance at a map of the world will show that although Lahore is on about the same latitude as Damascus, most of India lies nearer to the Equator than North Africa, and the southern tip of it very much nearer. Not only is this the case, but the great mountain barriers in the North shut in the whole country, so that it bears the appearance of two triangles of unequal size, the smaller standing upon the larger, which is just within the temperate zone, while the southern is within the tropics. From the northern mountains flow down great rivers, and it is hardly surprising that the inhabitants of the well-watered plains should have looked with awe at the vast and distant Himalayas, and should have believed that they contained the celestial home of the great and terrible god, Siva, as well as the centre of the world; while they held the huge stream of the Ganges, one of the four rivers flowing from the mythical Mount Kailas, to be most sacred, and of super-natural origin. Rising at a height of 13,000 feet, in a great ice-cavern, the Ganges flows for over a thousand miles through what is called Arya varta, the ancestral home of the Indian people. 'Mother Gunga'

1 Dr. Betty Heimann gives the figure as 1,581,410 square miles.

has stood indeed, throughout the ages, as the symbol of Divine beneficence. Small wonder that her children bathe in her waters by the thousand, and that upon her broad bosom their ashes are borne to their final resting-place. Small wonder that the towns and cities upon her banks are sacred, and that they form the chief places of pilgimage in the whole country. To die in Benares, it has been said, is to ensure one's salvation. Some devotees even make a six years' pilgrimage from the source of the Ganges to its mouth and back again, in order to expiate sin.

Between the Himalayas and the Vindhya, or 'divide' (a rocky and arid range of hills which separates the two triangles from one another), there lies a vast plain, two-and-a-half times the size of the British Isles. Here one half of the population of the entire Indian sub-continent finds its home—nearly 200 millions of people, mostly living in some 200,000 villages.

The southern peninsula has its largest population round the coastal areas, the interior being less densely inhabited.

India is the home of many physical types, and much of the oldest surviving stratum of the population bears a not inconsiderable resemblance to the Australian blackfellow. The very earliest inhabitants are now thought to have been negritos of the Andaman Island type, which survives in the Kadars and Uralis of the forests in the extreme South, and it is believed that the australoids came later. Primitive man certainly entered India at a very remote date, and may well have spread eastward through what we now call Indonesia, and have wandered as far as the Pacific. How much of the eastern area was then a mass of islands we do not know. Probably parts of it were not so deeply submerged, and may even have formed a continuous land-chain, joined up to the mainland of India.[2] The pre-history of the country has not yet been fully investigated, but the presence of stone implements and rock-paintings seems to suggest the presence at some distant period of peoples corresponding to the primitive culture of the so-called 'Aurignacians', whose art has been found in the Dordogne and Pyrenees, where it is dated at anything between 20,000 and 12,000 B.C.

Today only remnants of these ancient peoples survive in the hills and jungles of Central and Southern India, and they are either dying

2 The relation of India to the African continent is also obscure. Was there ever a junction between the two, of which Madagascar is now the main remnant? And why are folk tales in certain parts of India similar to some found in East Africa? Has there always been a western drift across the Indian Ocean?

out before the disturbing advance of civilisation, or are becoming absorbed into the social structure of Hinduism itself, and converted into Hindu castes. Their religion is either an almost pure pluralistic animism, or an animism modified by contact with the deities and doctrines of orthodox Hinduism. Typical of such peoples are the Chenchus and Baigas of the Central Provinces, or the Oraons[3] of Chota Nagpur. The 1941 census records about 180 primitive tribes.[4] Some of these are very small in numbers. Thus the Todas of the Nilgiri Hills are reckoned at 630 souls—a slightly larger number than ten years previously. The Sarunta of Bihar are numbered at only 188, and the Malapantaram of Travancore at 176, 104 males and seventy-two females. Other tribes, however, have a larger population. Thus the Bhils and the Gonds each number several millions.

*　　*　　*　　*　　*

In the year 1921 Sir John Marshall began his excavations in the Indus valley, first at Mohenjodaro in Sind, and then later at Harappa in the Western Punjab. His discoveries, a profusely illustrated account of which he published in three volumes in 1931, have revolutionised our conception of ancient history in general, and of the history of India in particular. The two sites which Marshall dug lie far apart, and it was sheer chance which led to the discovery of the ruins in these two places. Since then, remains of the same civilisation have been found as far apart as Kathiawar in the West and in the Ambala district of the Punjab, and there is reason to believe that it extended also to the Ganges valley. It was, therefore, not simply 'The civilisation of the Indus valley', but something which was widespread over large areas of India, especially in the North. And more than this, it was, as discovered, a highly-developed civilisation which must have taken a very long period indeed to arrive at the pitch demonstrated by these archæological finds. So, far from being a new and incipient thing, it was already 'age-old, and stereotyped on Indian soil, with many millenniums of human endeavour behind it'.[5]

Now the people who created this civilisation were not negritos or australoids, but early immigrants of a higher type. Their remains include statuettes, and from these and other artefacts we are led to infer that they are physically akin to the peoples who created the first beginnings of the Sumerian civilisation in Mesopotamia. It may

3 Although the latter speak a Dravidian language.
4 See the Government of India Census Report for 1941: Tables.
5 Nehru, op. cit. p. 47.

well be that both are branches of a common stock, perhaps originating somewhere in the regions round about what is now called Baluchistan; and it is probable that at a period ranging rather vaguely between 4,000 and 2,500 B.C. these people, either by sea or land, entered India and established themselves there, and that they spread right down into the southern tip of the lower triangle, and even into what is now Ceylon. Doubtless they intermarried with the so-called aborigines, the negritos and the australoids, and the resulting civilisation and breed of population thus contained a fusion of elements belonging to both the conquerors and the conquered.

The name by which these colonising people are usually known is 'Dravidian', and we can if we like call the early invaders 'proto-Dravidians'. The point of importance for our subject, however, is that right back in the days when Mohenjodaro and Harappa were flourishing cities, their citizens seen to have had a religion which already exhibited some of the elements familiar to observers of (say) nineteenth-century Hinduism. Thus a seal has been unearthed on which is depicted a horned figure seated in a cross-legged position, in all essentials similar to that in which the god Siva is often represented today. Horned cattle also appear to have been treated as sacred, just as they are today. Nagas or snake-spirits are believed in by these ancient dwellers in the Indus valley, and there is also a tree-cult, while a representation of a female vegetation-deity has been found.[6] Later invaders called these proto-Dravidians *sisna-devah* or phallus-worshippers, which suggests that their sanctuaries already contained the lingam or male symbol of fertility, which is another familiar accompaniment of the worship of Siva. These may seem slight pieces of evidence in themselves, and it must be confessed that so far no one has succeeded in deciphering the meaning of the Indus valley inscriptions,

6 It may startle some readers to think of ancient and long-standing elements in institutional Hinduism as allied to those which we are now finding to have existed in the Mediterranean and Asia Minor of antiquity, yet it is necessary to get accustomed to this. Not only is the megalithic culture of early India closely allied to what we discover to have prevailed in bronze-age Europe, including Britain, but the snake-cult of India has its parallels in Crete, and the bull-worshipping and bull-fighting practices of the early Mediterranean world have their counterparts in India, where, in the South, the Kallar have a popular sport of jumping on to an angry bull in order to pull off a cloth attached to its horns. Fire-walking ceremonies, also common in South India, were associated with the cult of Artemis in Cappadocia (*see* Prof. J. H. Hutton: *Caste in India*, p. 131). Hutton goes on to draw attention to the slender waists of males in Cretan paintings, which are very suggestive of medieval India—but this might be merely due to some kind of Mediterranean art infiltrating after Alexander, and in the time of Seleucus and his successors. The cult of snakes is a more serious parallel, since this appears alike in ancient Crete and in the Indus valley remains.

which are still as much an enigma to us as those of Etruria. Yet it may fairly be regarded as certain that there was not only a developed cultus, but that there has been no real breach of continuity between this early civilisation, and that obtaining in non-Moslem India at the time when the British occupation began.

Hinduism therefore, in certain major features, appears to be a much more ancient phenomenon than had previously been supposed, and since Southern India has been far less effectively overrun by invaders than the northern areas, it may well be that the rich developments in worship, devotion, literature, and architecture which are to be found there are more direct products of the culture and religion of early 'proto-Dravidian' India than we had previously thought.

This great civilisation did not, however, remain for ever undisturbed, though its persistence would mean that if it had had chronicles, they would have covered a more extended period than that which, in Roman history, separates the First Punic War from the fall of the Western Empire. In such a very long stretch of time there is ample room for all manner of important events and developments to have taken place: but as we see, until the ancient scripts can be read, and other excavations undertaken, the story of this past civilisation must remain concealed from us. What we do know is that somewhere in the region of 1700 B.C. waves of a fresh people began to cross over the North-West Frontier passes into the Punjab. We call these, for convenience, 'proto-Nordics'. They were, no doubt, folk of very much the same type as our Scandinavian and Anglo-Saxon forefathers, roving, vital, hard-fighting, heavy eaters and drinkers; and their religion was all of a piece with their character. Relatively they were barbarians, and they are supposed to have come from a kind of pool or breeding centre of this stock, somewhere in the neighbourhood of south-east Russia.[7] They spoke of themselves as *Aryas*, and the word is believed to be derived from a root connected with agriculture; but as they used it, it meant 'nobles', 'gentry', or 'aristocracy'.

These invaders spoke contemptuously of the dark-skinned folk whom they conquered, and called them Dasus or Dasyus, 'squat creatures' or 'slaves'—sometimes even 'apes'—and often referred to them as 'noseless'. This term of abuse plainly refers to the australoid feature of the nose with a concave bridge (technically known as

7 A last survival of these people in the form of the original stock which invaded India may be the red Kafirs of the North-West Frontier, who are reported by Hutton (op. cit. p. 38) as speaking a very early form of the Sanskrit language, using wooden vessels more suggestive of Scandinavia than of India, and tripods described as Grecian in type, and having lightish hair and eyes, tall stature and long heads.

platyrrhine), which is reproduced in many Indians of Dravidian stock, owing, no doubt, to cross-breeding with 'aborigines'. The Aryas made great efforts to keep their race pure, and the threefold division, primitive tribes, proto-Dravidians, and proto-Nordics, gives the obvious explanation of much that is connected with the origin and early development of the caste system. The word 'varna', which is used for some of the greater castes,[8] has to do with colour, and it may well be that one of the earliest divisions was between the conqueror and the conquered, and their different occupations.

Whatever obscurity may exist regarding the religion of the early Dravidians, that of the Aryas is at any rate something about which we can learn a certain amount, since it gave birth to a literature, and this consists largely of hymns or religious lyrics. The hymn is a devotional product of great antiquity, as Heiler has shown, and in oral transmission exists even now in backward areas of mankind in extremely primitive forms. More highly developed, it occurs in bulk in both ancient Egypt and Mesopotamia, and also in early China, and two types of it can be distinguished, the one, spontaneous and communal, and the other, literary, artificial, and individualistic.

The appearance of the articulate hymn represents a recognisable stage in the development of religious worship, and although at first it is no doubt only orally transmitted, partly because it is too sacred to be written down, and must be kept for the inner circle only, a stage is gradually reached at which a 'recording' is made of it, for the benefit (it would seem) of the sacred ministers, who must be scrupulously careful always to use exactly the same words, in order to ensure that the correct results follow. This, of course, is religion at the level of magic, and it plainly involves the idea that the deity addressed can be compelled by the correct formula to do what the worshipper desires. Whether this was the belief which evoked the hymns in the first instance we cannot now be certain, but at any rate it is clear that their collection and repetition at sacrifices soon becomes associated with this idea, and their preservation seems largely connected with the amassing of spells, charms, and formulas which will secure the proper sequence of the cosmic cycle, and fend off disturbances to the crops and cattle.[9]

8 But see Appendix to Chapter 2.

9 A somewhat similar fate befell the rather literary and individualistic hymns or Gathas in Iran, which tradition attributes to the prophet Zarathustra. Their preservation seems mainly due to their use (no doubt on account of the reverence with which they came to be regarded) either as charms or as powerful magical formulas. We need not suppose that these stereotyped hymns were necessarily used as charms in the higher stages of religion. As Professor Marsh has put it, they may have been used in order to demonstrate to the Deity that the worshipper understood what he was doing.

What sort of picture can we construct from these 'Vedic hymns', as they are called? What insight do they afford us into the lives and beliefs of the people who first spoke them? The answer to these questions I will try to give in the next chapter.

BOOKS FOR FURTHER STUDY

Cambridge History of India. Vol. I.

SIR JOHN MARSHALL. *Mohenjodaro and the Indus Civilisation.* 3 vols. London. 1931.

E. J. MACKAY. *The Indus Civilisation.* London. 1935.

2

THE RELIGION OF THE VEDIC AGE

The word *Veda* is a Sanskrit word. Sanskrit is the name of the ancient language of India, and means 'the cultured or aristocratic language', as distinct from Prakrit, 'the vulgar tongue'. Sanskrit was probably a living language up to the first centuries of the Christian era, and is closely allied, as might be expected, to ancient Persian or Iranian, since the Nordic invaders of India were a branch of the same people who, a little earlier, invaded Persia, and Iran and Arya are much the same words. The characters in which Sanskrit came to be written are derived from an old Semitic alphabet, similar to that used in certain Phoenician and Moabite tablets, but we do not know when writing first came into use in India. The Mohenjodaro inscriptions are not in the Sanskrit language. What seems certain is that long after writing was in common use, the literature which is called Vedic was still being handed down by word of mouth. Because it was sacred, it had to be kept secret, and was not allowed to be known or uttered by members of the lower castes, and it may not have been committed to writing until well after the time of Christ.

The word *Veda* is derived from a root, *vid*, to know, and is much the same as the Greek verb οἶδα. It means, in fact, knowledge, or transmitted wisdom, and the various Vedic books represent a collection of the knowledge of their age made for purposes of transmission. Hence they comprise a medley of many things, and even love potions. The Veda proper is divided into four books, the Rig-Veda or Royal Veda, which is made up of 1,028 hymns in ten sub-divisions; the Sama-Veda, which consists of selections of the same hymns specially arranged for chanting during sacrifice; the Yajur-Veda, which is liturgical prose, and the Atharva-Veda, which is a much more popular collection, and consists of charms and incantations (sacred sentences called *mantras*).

These four books are not really distinct productions, but overlap as to their text, very much as the four Gospels do. They are, in fact, four Samhitâs or collections of partly similar material, with varying additions, and the whole of the Sama-Veda, except seventy-five stanzas, is found in the Rig-Veda, while much of the Rig-Veda is also to be found in the Yajur-Veda and Atharva-Veda.

Appended to these four collections are others of a later date. These are called Brahmanas or priestly theorisings and instructions about the sacrificial ritual, and Upanishads or secret instructions about the meaning of the Vedic books themselves. The whole collection receives the title 'Veda', so that it has been said to include teaching upon three themes, ritual, prayer, and metaphysics.

With the Upanishads we shall be deeply involved in the next chapter. Here we are only concerned with the Vedas proper, and especially with the Rig-Veda. But it is by no means easy to deal wisely with so vast and varied a collection of literature, which is the accumulation of centuries, and which in any case may have been altered somewhat in the process of being written down. It may be almost as foolish to talk about 'the Vedic age' as about 'Bible times'.[1]

The Rig-Veda as a collection of hymns seems to have been closed as early as 800 B.C., since the Brahmanas, which assume its completeness, cannot be dated later than 800 to 600 B.C. It is essentially a collection of priestly upper-class literature, whereas the Atharva-Veda, although it contains some priestly material, is mainly a book of the religion of the common people.

Let us now try to gain some idea of the historical circumstances under which this literature came into being.

We must imagine the proto-Dravidian civilisation, with its subject aboriginal peoples, suddenly disturbed by the swarming in of proto-Nordic pioneers. The situation has been likened to the colonisation of North America by the white man, but it would be more correct to compare it with the conquest of Central America by the Spaniards, since the latter had to deal not only with semi-savage aborigines but with a rather highly developed urban culture, both in Mexico and Peru, having in each case a substantial history behind it. In the

1 It has been asserted by Professor Shastri that the earliest parts of the Vedas are the oldest records of the human mind anywhere in existence. But this can hardly be correct, if the present dating of the oldest Egyptian scripts be soundly based, since some of them are held to belong to the third or fourth millennium B.C. We may also have equally ancient literature in China and Sumeria.

eighteenth century B.C., the proto-Nordics were on the move in
northern Mesopotamia, and were settling in the Euphrates-Tigris
plains, and also in Persia, evidently actuated by a search for *lebensraum*;
and a certain amount of trade was passing between Bactria and the
Punjab. Nordic adventures may in this way have come to cross the
passes of the Hindu Kush, and to have brought back stories of the land
on the far side of it. There is no good reason for thinking of the actual
invasion as a single episode. On the contrary, it probably went on in a
series of tribal waves and settlements, some of them relatively peaceful,
others accompanied by armed force, and it may well have extended
over a period ranging from about 1700 to 1300 B.C.

Some of the Vedic poems indicate that the Dasyus or dark-skinned
inhabitants were not entirely subjugated, and that they may even have
acted as allies to groups of earlier Nordic settlers in their conflicts with
later and rival waves, just as, no doubt, British aborigines joined with
Anglo-Saxons to repel Danes. (It is now well recognised that the
British, so far from being entirely barbarians, were the possessors of
some arts and culture even before the Romans entered their country,
and the Romano-British were very likely more civilised than the
Anglo-Saxon-Jutish invaders, with whom they certainly intermarried.)
Dasyus and Aryas also intermarried, and in process of time their
religions may have syncretised to some degree. The result was the
adoption of the Vedic literature as the sacred property of both peoples,
but the conquerors treated it as too sacred to be imparted to persons
of a lower caste, while their subjects regarded it as possessing positively
magical properties.[2] One thing is certain, many of even the early
hymns of the Rig-Veda are not nearly as simple and naïve as might be
supposed. As we have received them, they are, in part at any rate, the
sophisticated products of a highly developed priesthood, and not by
any means entirely folk-poetry. A later generation came to call these
hymns *śruti* or revelation, 'that which has been heard'. Since, however,
most of them consist of lyrical addresses to the greater deities of the
people concerned, it is difficult to see what, in a literal sense, they
reveal. This, it seems, was soon realised, and in consequence, commentaries and allegorical interpretations had to be introduced, very
much as was done in regard to the Old Testament scriptures by the

2 The usual description by Hindus is that Vedic knowledge is infinite and eternal,
and that it comes to mankind intuitively by flashes of insight experienced by ancient
visionaries called Rishis, some of whom were men, some women. But this may seem
to some a rationalisation of the facts. Perhaps it would be safer, as in the case of the Bible,
to regard the elements of discovery and revelation, of the natural and the supernatural,
as blended together or intermingled.

early Christian Fathers. Yet, as originally spoken, these hymns were similar in form and sentiment to other early religious lyrics, such as Heiler has quoted in his great work on Prayer.

Two examples of Vedic hymns may here be given.[3] The first, addressed to Agni, the god of fire, represents him as the priest-attendant of the other gods, but also as of great benefit to mankind, bringing light and warmth, enabling men to work metals and so to grow rich, and doubtless also making it possible to cook food.

> I praise Agni, the chosen priest, god, minister of sacrifice, the hotar, lavishest of wealth.
> Worthy is Agni to be praised by living as by ancient seers; he shall bring hitherward the gods.
> Through Agni man obtaineth wealth, yea plenty, waxing day by day;
> Most rich in heroes, glorious.
> Agni, the perfect sacrifice which thou encompassest about verily goeth to the gods.
> May Agni, sapient-minded priest, truthful, most gloriously great,
> The god, come hither with the gods.
> Whatever blessing, Agni, thou wilt grant unto the worshippers, that, Angiras, is thy truth, indeed.
> To thee, dispeller of the night, O Agni, day by day with prayer bringing thee reverence, we come.
> Ruler of sacrifices, guard of law eternal, radiant one, increasing in thine own abode.
> Be to us easy of approach, even as a father to his son; Agni, be with us for our weal.

The second hymn, entitled 'to Indra' (god of the thundercloud), is actually a chieftain's drinking song—one of the finest of its kind in the world,—and it is implied that Indra himself is the speaker—a super-warrior, arrogant and half-intoxicated.

> Thus indeed, thus is my mind: kine and horses will I win.
> > Have I not drunk of the Soma?—
> Like the roaring winds the draughts of Soma have roused me up.
> > Have I not drunk of the Soma?—
> The draughts have roused me up, as swift horses a chariot.
> > Have I not drunk of the Soma?—
> The hymn has drawn nigh to me, as a lowing cow to her dear calf.
> > Have I not drunk of the Soma?—

3 The translation of the first hymn is by Dr. Nicol MacNicol, the second by Dr. E. J. Thomas.

As a carpenter making a seat for the chariot, round my heart I bend the
hymn.
      Have I not drunk of the Soma?—
In no wise are the five peoples aught to me.
      Have I not drunk of the Soma?—
Not the half part of me are both worlds (Heaven and earth)
      Have I not drunk of the Soma?—
The Heaven have I overpassed in greatness and his great earth.
      Have I not drunk of the Soma?—
Lo! I will put down this earth here or yonder.
      Have I not drunk of the Soma?—
Swiftly will I smite the earth here or yonder.
      Have I not drunk of the Soma?—
In Heaven is one half of me. Down below I have drawn the other.
      Have I not drunk of the Soma?—
I am most mighty. Nigh to the clouds have I risen.
      Have I not drunk of the Soma?—
I go to the house of him that is ready. To the gods goes the oblation-bearer.
      Have I not drunk of the Soma?

And now for the picture. The Aryas are ceasing to be nomads, but
are becoming an agricultural rather than an urbanised people. They
know about barley, which they grow and use, presumably much as
the Tibetans do today. Their chief weapon is the bow, which is
apostrophised in one of the greater hymns (as apparently it was also
by the Hebrews[4]), and which was evidently regarded by them with
supernatural awe as containing what a Polynesian would call *mana*.
They are warlike and restless in disposition. They are heavy eaters and
drinkers, and they are acquainted with a species of alcohol (Soma)
which they hold sacred. They are at first grouped into five tribes
(though these disappear by coalescence at a late date), and each tribe
has its prince or chieftain. The ruling class are called Kshatriyas or
warriors. Kingship is hereditary, and so is priesthood, which, even at
the time of the entry into India, is fully developed. The oldest account
gives several different sorts of priest, but the chief of these is the *hotar*,
who composed and recited the sacred hymns. Each prince had a
domestic chaplain or family priest, called a *purohita*, and the *purohit* as
a class survives to this day! The priest received a *dakshina* or fee for
properly performing the sacrifice, and sometimes the gift was very
large.

    The divine powers believed in and worshipped by these early Nordic

4 *See* 2 Sam.i.18 (R.V.)

colonists are Powers of Nature in the first instance, and there is to begin with no idea of a single supreme Godhead. Indeed the primary notion seems to be that of a plurality of Powers, not even personal ones, but connected with the various objects, occurrences or episodes of daily life. The name of the thing or the circumstance is the name of the god. Thus Agni is Fire, and then gradually He of the Fire. Ushas is Dawn, and then gradually She of the Dawn. Soma is an intoxicating drink, and later the divinity who can induce exalted states of consciousness. It is only as the physical basis of this divinity tends to be forgotten that the god comes to be fully personified. Sometimes the same object is given several names, corresponding to different occasions. Thus the sun has six different titles, corresponding to position and functions, while the lightning has seven. It is hardly surprising that this implied plurality of beings should tend towards fusion. Although there is division of labour among the gods, there is in addition a good deal of overlapping. There are also demons, who represent the grim and hostile forces of nature. Some of the minor divinities such as Aranyi, She of the Wild Wood, look like loans from the pantheon of the people who were conquered. *Aranyi* means 'jungle', and is therefore simply the spirit worshipped by the jungle tribes. As such she is worshipped today by people like the Chenchus, who say she may be met as an old woman walking in the woods. Trees and plants, too, as worshipped in the Vedic period and later, may be the same as those venerated by the proto-Dravidians of the pre-Vedic period. Yet it has been inferred that the Aryas brought a good many of their gods with them, since the names of divinities found on inscriptions in Asia Minor are the same as those of divinities referred to in the Vedic hymns.[5]

The departed ancestors have their portion in this religion. Cremation is the common way of disposing of the dead, though ordinary earth-burial seems to have preceded it. Perhaps it was the Dravidians who practised the latter, and the Aryas who cremated, since if you are a nomad on trek, it is more natural to dispose of your dead by burning them in the camp-fire, and also prevents any ill-disposed person from mishandling the corpse. The Hindu service of the dead known as *sraddha* has its roots in the Vedic period, and the offering of food and drink to the departed is here, just as much as in China, a stable feature of filial piety (and is known as *pitri-puja*—*pitri*= Lat. *patres*).

It is said that in the Rig-Veda there is no idea of transmigration of of souls or of re-birth. A future Paradise full of felicity is prepared for the blessed dead, and there is evidence, less abundant, but quite

5 *See* note to Varuna.

convincing, that evil-doers were believed to go to a different sort of place, a kind of bottomless pit. Early ancestors of renown, the Pitris or Fathers, were venerated, and were believed to share with the Deva or greater gods in the benefit of the sacrifices, just as they did in China in the sacrifices at the Altar of Heaven. Paradise is represented as the reward for valour in battle (cf. the Norse Valhalla), for generous gifts to the priesthood (was this a Dravidian addition?), and for austerity amassing merit. There are, however, in the tenth book of the Rig-Veda, which contains late hymns, two passages which vaguely suggest the idea of re-birth. The conclusion must be that although it was not an integral part of the natural belief of the Aryas, it developed in India itself for some unascertained reason, towards the end of the Vedic period.

The one great problem in the religion of the Rig-Veda is the god called Varuna. The name itself is fairly straightforward. It is plainly similar to the Greek word Ouranos, which means the encircling heaven above, and presumably meant in the beginning: 'He of the Sky'. In Greek mythology Zeus (or Dyaus) and Ouranos are related, the latter being the ancestor of the former, and Zeus being 'the bright sky'. Dyaus also appears among the Vedic gods, where he is the great Parent of the devas, and is associated with Prthivi, Mother Earth, as his consort. But whereas among the Greeks Zeus retains and even increases his importance, in India Ouranos or Varuna[6] becomes the great personality, and what is still more remarkable, Varuna for a time ceases to be merely 'the Man in the sky', and becomes very nearly the sole Supreme Being, invested with intense moral holiness, and always displaying interest in the moral order of the world (its *rita*), rewarding virtue and punishing transgressions, merciful and gracious, all-seeing and all-wise, the Creator and the Ruler of the cosmic scheme.

Thus in Book i, hymn 25,[7] we read:

Whatever law of Thine, O god, O Varuna, as we are men,
Day after day we violate,
Give us not as a prey to death, to be destroyed by thee in wrath,
To Thy fierce anger when displeased.

6 Varuna appears as a god in the earliest Vedic literature, and some have thought him to be a survival from an early pre-Vedic period of proto-Nordic monotheism. But there is no positive evidence for this. All we know is that the name occurs in an inscription of about 1300 B.C. found at Boghaz Keui in Asia Minor, and presumably connected with some proto-Nordics who invaded that area.

7 MacNicol, *Hindu Scriptures*, p. 4.

Varuna, true to holy law, sits down among his people; he Most wise, sits
there to govern all.
From thence perceiving, he beholds all wondrous things, both what hath
been
And what hereafter will be done.

and again in Book v, hymn 85[8]:

If we have sinned against the man who loves us, have ever wronged a
brother, friend, or comrade,
The neighbour ever with us, or a stranger, O Varuna, remove from us the
trespass.

If we as gamesters cheat at play, have cheated, done wrong unwittingly or
sinned of purpose,
Cast all these sins away like loosened fetters, and Varuna, let us be thine
own beloved.

How could this spiritual promotion have come about? It is thought
by some that the conception of Varuna has been enhanced by the drift
of ideas from Iran, where Zarathustra had preached a high monotheism.
In Iran the names of Dyaus and Ouranos or Varuna completely disappear, and their place is taken by that of Ahuramazda, the Wise Lord.
It is indeed possible that the attributes of Ahuramazda were transferred
in Vedic India to Varuna, with the results above mentioned. Others
think that Hebrew prophetic influence may have been at work, but
it is difficult to be sure of the dating, and Varuna as an ethical god
may well be earlier than the age of Amos or of Isaiah.[9] The matter is
still obscure, and recent research has shown the beginnings of a similar
ethical monotheism in very ancient Egypt—perhaps as far back as the
fourth millennium B.C., while as recently as the early nineteenth
century A.D. a kind of independent growth of ethical monotheism has
been recorded in an inland province of Japan, where it was due to the
prophetic ministry of a Shintoist farmer. It is therefore unnecessary to
suppose that India could not have produced a tendency to a similar
movement as early as the middle of the Vedic period. What remains
as a disappointment is the failure of the Varuna cult to develop, and to
culminate in a complete triumph for transcendent monotheism.
Varuna, in spite of his temporary eminence, always remains associated
with a group of gods called Adityas, similar to one another in function

8 MacNicol, op. cit. p. 19.
9 Griswold. *The Religion of the Rig-Veda.* Chapter 5.

C

and style—Mitra, Aryaman, Parjanya, Bhaga, Daksa, and Amsa (though the number is sometimes increased to twelve). This presents an analogy to what is found in the Iran of Zarathustra's day, where Ahuramazda is surrounded by a group of angelic beings or inferior divinities, called Ameshaspentas. But in India, however much Varuna may be exalted, the other Adityas are never degraded to the level of creaturely beings, as the Ameshaspentas seem to have been in Iran, while after some centuries Varuna ceases any longer to be treated as a great ethical god, and sinks to the level of a mere tutelary divinity of the waters. This decline in status is lamentable. It seemed at one point as though Varuna might become what has been termed 'a Rig-Vedic Yahweh, set over against the world'. But in Iran and in India the movements of thought went different ways. Anthropogeographers will no doubt attribute this to differences in climate or food or soil, and Marxists to differences in economic conditions. At any rate in India thought went in a pantheistic direction, rather than in that of a transcendent monotheism, and Varuna thus became 'a second-rate Neptune de-ethicised, and almost depersonalised', his place being taken first by Indra, who is a frankly non-moral nature-deity, subsequently by the impersonal Brahma, who is 'beyond good and evil', and who *is* the world, immanent in all beings, and later still by Vishnu and Siva.

The time seems eventually to have arrived when no more substantial migrations of Nordics came over the Hindu Kush. The demand for *lebensraum* had evidently been satisfied; the swarming period was over for the time being; and those who had come, for weal or woe, remained in India to make it their permanent home. They were now isolated from their homeland, wherever it may have been, and had to adjust themselves to the climate and social conditions of the country of their adoption.

It has often been asserted by quite responsible thinkers, Albert Schweitzer, for instance, that Indian differs profoundly from European and Transatlantic thought, because of the great part in it which is played by 'world and life-negation'. We shall come to grips with this feature in the next and subsequent chapters, but of the period pictured in the Rig-Veda, at any rate in its earlier poems, world-negation does not seem a prominent feature. The Aryas, on the contrary, seem to be a world-affirming and joyous set of people. Austerity, as mentioned above, exists, but it may well be an element belonging to the proto-Dravidian culture, and there it may have taken a long time to develop, and even then may have existed side by side with a large measure of life-affirmation. It is possible that it is more congenial to the dark-white than to the fair Nordic, since it is probable that the bulk of the members of the monastic orders in Europe today are persons who have a strong dark-white strain in their make-up. Yet as far as India herself is concerned, Pandit Nehru maintains[10] that at every period when her civilisation bloomed we find 'an intense joy in life and nature, a pleasure in the act of living, a development of art and music and literature, of song, dancing, painting, and the theatre, and even a highly sophisticated inquiry into sex-relations'. He thinks it inconceivable that a view of life based on world-worthlessness could have produced all these manifestations of vigorous and varied life, spread over many centuries. How is it then that India has acquired the reputation of being essentially the home of world-renunciation?

India has for centuries been at the mercy of epidemic disease. In the twenty-five years following 1896, 10,000,000 died there from bubonic plague alone. Over 7,000,000 die annually from fever. In Bengal 350,000 to 400,000 die annually of malaria, the latter disease accounting for 200,000,000 days of sickness per annum. In large areas 80 per cent of the population are afflicted with parasitic hook-worm. All this, coupled with widespread famines and droughts, tends to lower the vitality of the people. It may well be that climatic and economic conditions in a country which, as we have seen, is largely tropical have produced in those who have to endure them a certain world weariness, and so a readiness to adopt a world-negating attitude, and that this tendency affects all comers. Certainly it is true that Englishmen who have spent long years in India, if they have sensitive natures, not infrequently find themselves caught up into this frame of mind.

But a caveat must be entered here. Many have come to think that because the great literature of the post-Vedic periods is full of the *motif* of abstention from life, because the only India known to visitors from the West is so full of ascetics, and because the national hero for many years has been himself an ascetic, therefore the world-negating attitude is the *only* attitude possible to Indians, the only one they can admire, and the only one which can ever be characteristic of them. This is a rash assumption. Suppose that we ourselves could be transported back to the medieval Europe of the twelfth and thirteenth centuries, with its tradition of monasticism and eremitism stretching back for some 800 years. We should find vast multitudes of monks and nuns, and in the City of London alone, an anchorite (very much like an Indian ascetic or *sadhu*) in every parish, almost in every street. We might

10 Op. cit. p. 58.

suppose, if we did not know what was to follow (with the Renaissance and our own age of scientific humanism), that no other feeling about life was possible except that of medieval Christianity.

It is true that in certain periods of Indian history there was a running away from life on a big scale, as for example in the hey-day of the Buddhist movement. But so there was in Egypt in the fourth century after Christ, when the trek into the desert was called ἀποχώρησις, and again in the Dark Ages, the times of St. Radegund and St. Etheldreda. The causes were sometimes over-taxation, sometimes depressing political, social, or economic conditions, and especially in early medieval Europe, the break-up of settled Roman provincial government, and the horrors of barbarism. A Russian journalist who had travelled in Central Asia told the author not long ago that the great attraction of monasticism for the Tibetan was the freedom from the pressure of economic problems which it gave to the individual.[11]

It is right to recognise the enormous part which austerity and world-renunciation have played in Indian life and thought, from the days of Gautama to those of Gandhi, but it does not follow that in a self-governing India, with the ten-year programme of the National Planning Committee fully realised, and much more ample and efficient welfare services adequately maintained over a substantial period, there would necessarily be the same attitude to life. As it is, there is evidence that for some 1,300 years there were in existence great states in Southern (and that is to say, tropical) India, which not only displayed a rich and complex culture of a world-affirming character, but which also engaged in immense colonising activities, and extended their sway as far as what is now called Indonesia.

We must now pass on to consider the great and momentous developments in India's religious life which occurred approximately between 800 B.C. and the Christian era.

APPENDICES TO CHAPTER 2

CASTE:

As there will be many references to the latter during the course of this book, it seems advisable to interrupt the narrative at this point, and leaving the historical sequence, to offer some definitions of caste and its accompaniments. The name itself was given to the whole

---

11 In the days when no social security and pension schemes existed, monasticism may have been a convenient way of disposing of widows, surplus spinsters, elderly misfits, and invalids. In a warm climate old men may be more comfortable in the jungle than in a crowded hut, where they and the younger folk are getting on one another's nerves.

system by the first Portuguese colonists (Latin, *castus*, pure: but the word in Portuguese does not mean this, but 'breed', and is perhaps derived from another root. If not, it must mean 'pure-bred').[12]

Although analogies to caste have been detected by observers in many countries, from ancient Egypt to modern South Africa and America, it seems best to use Furnival's generic term, 'a plural society', to describe all these different phenomena, and to say that the peculiarly complicated type of plural society which we encounter in India is the product of many centuries of immigration and geographical isolation. It is a social rather than a religious phenomenon, though the effects of the system are to be seen in religion. For example, the length of time of purification is longer in some castes than in others, and lower castes have in the past been forbidden to read the Vedas, or even to listen to their recitation.

The word for caste in India is 'varna'[13] so far as the four main castes are concerned, and 'jati' for the others. 'Varna' means colour, 'jati' means rank, birth, or lineage. It is thus evident that the earliest phase of the caste system resulted from the conquest of one people by another of a different skin-colouring, and this would be the case even if caste existed among the Dravidians, since the australoid and negrito inhabitants would have been darker still,[14] although it would have greater significance as between blond Nordics and brown Dravidians. When division of functions and specialisation increased, the new classes took the form of castes. At first, such classes were in a fluid condition at the lower end. Rigidity came later. The old divisions were into five grades: Brahmins (priests), Kshatriyas (warriors), Vaisyas (merchants, or earlier, agriculturalists), Sudras (artisans and later land-workers) and Pariahs (outsiders). The addition of vast numbers (sometimes over 2,000) of minor castes, either occupational, or due to conquest, and the effects of colonisation, or the assimilation by Hinduism of some primitive non-Hindu people—all these have enormously complicated the system. Finally the general belief in re-birth has meant that some religious teachers have encouraged the idea that transgression may involve being born in a lower caste, and that merit may lead, conversely, to promotion in the next stage of reappearance on earth. Side by side with this, and inconsistent with it, is the doctrine that caste is a kind of predestined order, and that by no sort of device can one be

12 *See* Hutton, op. cit. p. 42.

13 *Varna*, according to Hutton, is now better taken to mean 'group', since a *varna* may include more than a single caste.

14 The Indian term of abuse, 'noseless', would seem to indicate the existence of an australoid feature in plebeian stock. It does not mean, as in Shakespeare's day, 'syphilitic'.

changed from one caste to another while one lives. Caste, on this view is hereditary, and all persons have 'to keep their proper stations'. No one is permitted to eat or drink with a person who is not of his own caste, nor may he marry outside it, even if he falls in love. Although the caste-divisions still exist, they do not now invariably determine the avocation of the individual. Thus Brahmins may be found who are doctors or lawyers, not priests; and many Kshatriyas are not in any army. There are also some strange anomalies, such as a servant of high caste (e.g. a Brahmin cook) working for a mistress of low caste, and a ruler of a native sovereign state who is of low-caste origin, high rank and high caste not being synonymous. Some ancient castes correspond to occupations which in the West would land a person in prison. Thus there is actually a caste of burglars or highwaymen, who have even a tutelary goddess, to whom they make offerings before committing a crime.

It is, however, significant that again and again public esteem has been seen to light upon an individual who possesses outstanding qualities of learning or virtue, rather than upon one who possesses the necessary caste qualifications without such moral or intellectual qualities. Gandhiji was not a Brahmin but a Vaisya, and a number of outcastes have been revered as saints.

(For a very full discussion of caste in all its bearings, see J. H. Hutton, *Caste in India*, Cambridge University Press, 1946.)

THE BRAHMINS:

There is no other country in the whole world which has developed so extraordinary an institution as the Brahmin caste. It is as though (to give a rough analogy) the Roman Catholic hierarchy in Spain or Ireland were to be allowed to marry, with the hereditary right of the children of such marriages to succeed their parents in official status. Eliot defines the Brahmins as 'an hereditary guild possessing secret professional knowledge'. The word should strictly be spelt *Brahman*, but since, unfortunately, this word is also used as an epithet of the Supreme Being, it is confusing to employ it in reference to mortals, and the old-fashioned form *Brahmin*, though incorrect, is more serviceable. The word *Brahman* is used of priests in the Rig-Veda, as well as of deities (there is, for instance, one passage in which Agni is addressed as *Brahman*). The probability is that the word, whatever its etymology, may signify something like our word 'divine', which, as a noun, is usable in reference to a clergyman, while as an adjective it is applicable to God. The word in the Rig-Veda has just this significance. It means a priest, not a particular class or grade of priests. Originally there may not have been a differentiated priesthood among the proto-Nordic invaders, though it is more likely, from what we know of the general habits and customs of the dark-whites of whom the Dravidians were a branch, that they themselves did possess one, and that the institution may have got worked into the social structure of the invaders as they settled down.[15] But the periodically displayed rivalry between the Kshatriyas and the Brahmins would seem to suggest that the development of a sacerdotal caste in higher circles did not go on without challenge.

The Brahmins are not an exact counterpart of either Christian or Moslem clergy, since, in a sense, they make the doctrinal formularies and frame the canons without being bound by them. They can be as lax or as liberal in their theology as they like, and with perfect impunity. No one dare question their authority. They are, in fact, as Eliot says in another place, 'an intellectual hereditary aristocracy, who claim to direct the thought of India, no matter what forms it may take'.[16] Nehru, who is himself a Kashmiri Brahmin, repeats this in other words. 'The task,' he says, 'of determining values, and the preservation of ethical standards, was allotted to a class or group of thinkers who were freed from material cares, and were, as far as possible, without obligations, so that they could consider life's problems in a spirit of detachment. This class was supposed to be at the top of the social structure, honoured and respected by all.'[17] Such a definition gives the Brahmins the same kind of status and prestige as that possessed by the Victorian university don in relation to the townspeople of either Oxford or Cambridge. But Nehru goes on to admit that in addition to this, the Brahmins became a powerful and entrenched priesthood, intent on preserving their vested interests, and that they have, as such, shown in the past all the vices of a privileged class, while large numbers of them have possessed neither learning nor virtue. Yet he thinks that in spite of this they have held their own in public favour, partly because they have produced a remarkable succession of men of intelligence, partly because their record of public service has been notable. It may be objected that this is an inevitably biased opinion, yet, as Dr. Inge has reminded us, intellectual ability is remarkably heritable.

Whether the institution of Brahminism will be able to survive the

15 Some have sought to trace a philological connexion between the Latin *flamen* and the Sanskrit *brahmin*, on the basis of Grimm's law.
16 Op. cit. vol. i, p. 17.
17 Op. cit. p. 61.

radical changes which are now obviously impending in India may be doubted. Certainly Marxist influences would be completely hostile to its continuance.[18]

Although every Brahmin possesses the hereditary qualification for the priestly office, not every Brahmin exercises it. The vocation, he feels, is overcrowded, or he may perhaps know of a more congenial or lucrative way of living. A fairly large liberty is allowed him, so long as he avoids ceremonial pollution. Hence Brahmins in considerable numbers are to be found in the army, the police, the civil service, and the professions, as well as in ordinary clerkships. They will engage in farming, so long as they can hire labour for the menial tasks. In 1909 it was found that in Bengal proper, one in six, in Bihar one in thirteen, and in Orissa only one in thirty-six, was acting as a priest. Probably the proportions have further diminished since then.[19]

DISTINGUISHING MARKS:

   (1) caste   (2) sectarian   (3) married women

Not perhaps in the earliest period, but certainly for many centuries, it has been an obligation, or at least a custom, to designate one's membership of one of the four main castes, or one's adherence to one of the chief religious sects, by an external and visible symbol, marked somewhere on the body.

According to the laws of Manu[20] (q.v.) the four caste-marks run thus:

The colouring of such marks on the forehead varies with the caste: white for Brahmins, red for Kshatriyas, yellow for Vaisyas, and black for Sudras. The exact form prescribed for such marks varies however in the different authorities.

Their significance will be better understood after Chapter 6 has been read. Sectarian marks also vary. Broadly speaking, the mark for a devotee of Vishnu is Ɣ , which some say represents the god's footmark, but the different sub-sects of Vaishnavites vary it a good deal, so that it assumes among others the following forms:

---

18 Though Marxism is quite capable of creating a new sort of dominant caste as in Russia.

19 For some account of sacrificial duties, *see* Chapter 9, p. 140 ff.

20 *See* p. 72.

The sectarian mark for Saivites is usually three horizontal lines: ≋ which are smeared not only on the forehead, but also on the arms and breast. Here again there are some variations: ⊞ ≋ ⚇ • the last being for a devotee of Sakta, the female principle in Saivism. These marks seem usually to be white or yellow.

Sometimes, in addition, the devotee carries a symbol such as a *lingam* or a *nandi* (Saivite bull) on the head, after the manner of a crest.

It has been suggested that the use of sectarian marks may not have been unknown to the ancient Mediterranean world, since we have the examples of the so-called Phrygian cap among devotees of Mithras, while Apuleius, in his 'Golden Ass', seems to suggest that an Isiac devotee also had some sort of badge on the body; and there is also the curious reference in Revelation xiv to the mark of the Beast which was worn on the foreheads of those who venerated the Divine Cæsar. But no evidence is available as to what this was like.

Zealous Jews, on the other hand, certainly used to obey literally the command to bind a scroll of the law as a frontlet between the eyes and also on the left arm, and this phylactery, as it is called in New Testament Greek (Aramaic, *tephillim*), must have looked very much like some of the head ornaments worn by Hindus. Jews also had distinguishing fringes (*tsitsith*) to the borders of their garments (see Numbers xv, 37).

Orthodox Hindus are specially distinguished by their top-knot, or lock of hair which is worn long on the apex of the skull, often with the rest of the crown close-shaven.

The crimson dot (or *tīlaka*) on a woman's forehead is a sign that she is married, and implies her subjection to her husband, who stands to her as the representative of deity, and is often treated by his wife on rising in the morning with certain ceremonies which imply such a status. It is curious to reflect that the opposite of this is shown in the Christian form of marriage (see the *Book of Common Prayer*), where the *man*, in placing the ring on the woman's finger, says: 'With my body I thee worship.' The Puritans in 1604 and 1661 actually raised objection to this, and the word has been altered in the 1928 book to 'honour'.

(For a very full account of the sectarian marks, with coloured illustrations showing all the variations, reference may be made to a monograph published by the Municipal Corporation of the City of Bombay, and written by Mr. D. A. Pai, Assistant Curator and Secretary, Victoria and Albert Museum, Bombay.)

BOOKS FOR FURTHER STUDY

H. D. GRISWOLD. *The Religion of the Rig-Veda*. Oxford. 1923.

PROFESSOR A. BERRIEDALE KEITH. *The Religion and Philosophy of the Veda*. Cambridge, Mass. 1925. Harvard Oriental Series.

PROFESSOR J. H. HUTTON. *Caste in India*. Cambridge. 1946.

3

THE AGE OF THE UPANISHADS

Oriental scholars are in the habit of telling us that our European custom of limiting studies to Greek, Hebrew, and Latin literature has given us merely a Mediterranean picture of the world. This may well be so, and it is no doubt a pity that Sanskrit and Chinese seem so hard to the European student, who must needs depend mainly upon translations of Eastern classics. Professor E. R. Dodds has drawn attention to 'the oriental background against which Greek culture arose, and from which it was never completely isolated save in the minds of classical scholars'.[1] These considerations matter a good deal when we come to consider the very remarkable literature referred to in the title of this chapter.

Greeks, Indians, Chinese and Iranians have this in common, as against the highly industrialised people of Europe and America in the twentieth century, that whereas the latter are chiefly obsessed with the notion that the really important thing is to be comfortable, the former are, in *their* golden age, for ever seeking a religion and a fundamental theory of life which will give them poise and harmony of mind amid circumstances which are often uncomfortable and always disappointing.

Somewhere in the region of 800 B.C. North India witnessed the beginnings of a great development in Indo-Aryan thought.

The Aryas themselves had now been settled down for a long time, and a prosperous and fairly stable order of society had grown up in which, under various independent and neighbouring rulers, the new and the old were blended into one. Aryan thought and ideals were dominant, but there was a background containing older elements of

1 *Humanism and Technique in Greek Studies* (1936), p. 11.

belief and worship as well, derived from the stocks which had been subjugated. What is noticeable, however, is that although the Vedic hymns are still quoted with respect, they are no longer treated literally, but figuratively, allegorically, and sometimes even ironically. The gods of the Rig-Veda are no longer felt satisfying in many circles as genuine objects of belief, and the ritual of the priests is beginning to be ridiculed. All this sounds very much like what happened in Hellas a few centuries later under Xenophanes and his successors. Sceptical inquiry and philosophy were beginning to compete with naïve religion. Man in India was coming, as elsewhere, to a transitional stage between highly developed ritual sacrifice (with the belief in gods many and lords many, of a quasi-human character), and a religion built on an entirely different basis.

It must not be overlooked that there was an intermediary stage between this new movement and the age of the early Rig-Veda hymns. This was the stage of the Brahmanas. The latter are directions and explanations connected with the due performance of the sacrificial ritual. Sacrifice had hitherto been a personal approach to a quasi-human deity for the purpose of securing his or her favour by offering a gift, usually of food. The offering naturally grew stereotyped by repetition, and it was considered important to make it 'decently and in order'. Hence rubrical instructions grew up, of a very detailed and often complicated character. In the Brahmanas we see these rubrical matters becoming almost an end in themselves. The ceremonial is more and more detached from its connexion with the personal deity who is on any specific occasion the object of address, and becomes *cosmic* ceremonial, necessary for the carrying on of the cosmic processes; and the result of this is to dethrone the gods from their ultimacy, and to pave the way for the rise of some more metaphysical type of religion, either an impersonal monism, or pluralism, or even a sort of theism. For the time being it merely produces the impression upon us, as Sir Charles Eliot has put it, that the one chief occupation of India must have been the performance with meticulous accuracy of the most complicated forms of ritual. (It is perhaps worth remarking that this artificial ritualism still persists in many orthodox Hindu circles,[2] though with diminishing regularity, and its future now seems precarious, although its performance represents a considerable element in the daily life of an observant member of the priestly or Brahmin caste.) What happened about 800 B.C. was the rise of an influential minority

2 *See* in this book, Chapter 9, section 4a.

movement which began to declare that it was both unnecessary and futile.

It must not be supposed that the transition from naïve worship to sophisticated ritualism and from ritualism to sceptical inquiry was at all clear-cut. It hardly touched great masses of Indians, and to this day Hinduism, as we shall see, is extremely tolerant of this old ritual for those who feel its attraction. The situation is rather as though an English farmer, though himself not a very regular churchgoer, and perhaps a bit of an agnostic, were to argue that unless the full cycle of devotional exercises in the *Book of Common Prayer* were properly carried out by his vicar, the crop would not grow, and the cattle would be sickly; and that prayers for rain and fine weather must be duly offered as part of the technique for securing them, even though belief in the Apostles' Creed might be more or less abandoned. The leaders of thought, however, in the period we are now considering were inclined to go beyond such compromises. There was, in fact, a criticism of objective sacrifice, resembling, though not identical with, similar criticisms which have arisen in other parts of the world, and which we find in Hebrew prophetism, Chinese ethical wisdom, and European Protestantism. Together with this criticism went also a flight from the artificialities of contemporary civilisation. Some of the literature of the movement bears the title of Aranyakas, or 'forest books', and it is clear that the name indicates a situation in which earnest and spiritually minded people left home and its complicated amenities and duties, and went into the jungle. There they meditated, and gathered disciples whom they instructed in what seemed to them the true way of life, and debated with them on the basic meaning of the world. It is a record of these instructions and debates that makes up a large part of the literature which we shall now consider.

Philosophising in India begins very far back.

Even in the earlier Rig-Veda (Book i, hymn 164) occurs a *brahmodya* or theological riddle ascribed to the *rishi* Dirghatamas, in which occurs the verse which is often quoted as the actual beginning of all Indian philosophy:

> *Indram Mitram Varunam Agnim ahur*
> *Atho divyah sasuparno Garutman*
> *Ekam sad vipra bahudha vadamti,*
> *Agnim Yaman Matarisvanam ahuh.*

> They call it Indra, Mitra, Varuna, and Agni,
> And also heavenly, beauteous-winged Garutman:

> The Real is One, though sages name it variously,—
> They call it Agni, Yama, Matarisvan.

In the later portions of the Rig-Veda occur hymns such as the 129th in the tenth book:

> Non-being then existed not, nor being,
> There was no air, nor sky which is beyond it;
> What was concealed?—Wherein?—In whose protection?—
> And was there deep unfathomable water?—

> Death then existed not, nor life immortal;
> Of neither night nor day was any token;
> By its inherent force the One breathed breathless;
> No other thing than that beyond existed.

> Darkness there was at first, by darkness hidden;
> Without distinctive mark this all was water;
> That which, becoming, by the void was covered,
> That One, by force of heat (tapas) came into being.

> Desire entered that One in the beginning,—
> Desire that was the earliest seed of mind.
> The ages seeking in their hearts with wisdom,
> Found out the bond of being in non-being.

> Their ray extended light across the darkness;
> But was the One above, or was it under?—
> Creative force was there and fertile power,
> Below was energy, above was impulse.

> Who knows for certain?—Who shall here declare it?—
> Whence was it born, and whence came this creation?—
> The gods were born after this world's creation;
> Then who can know from whence it has arisen?—

> Wherefrom then this creation has arisen,
> And whether He has or has not produced it,—
> He who surveys it in the highest heaven,
> He only knows, or even He may not.[3]

3 This creation hymn, which is here given in Professor Macdonell's translation, is perhaps the most remarkable in the whole of the Rig-Veda. It is tempting to speculate whether any of this wisdom of the sages owes its origin to thinkers in the pre-Vedic stage of Indian history, the records of which have so far proved impossible to unravel. Were we to suppose a link between the Sumerians and the peoples of the Indus valley, it might be possible to conjecture some connexion (due to common materials) between the Babylonian-Jewish hymn of Creation which we find in Genesis I and the hymn quoted above. But all this is a matter of utter obscurity, and in the absence of evidence one must refrain from dogmatic assertion.

Such compositions are really more characteristic of the age of philosophy proper, but the line is not at all sharply drawn, and some of the older philosophical treatises themselves are integral parts and continuations of the Brahmanas, while in several of these treatises matter is included which is much more akin to the substance of the ritual Brahmanas themselves, and conversely, material which is definitely labelled as Brahmanic is philosophical in character. Later on, however, a distinct class of independent philosophical and theological treatises arose, which had no connexion at all with the books of ritual.

It is these philosophical and theological treatises, separate and combined, which bear the name of Upanishads. The word Upanishad is derived from a verb 'to sit down opposite somebody' (upa = near + ni = down + sad = to sit). It means therefore first 'the act of sitting close to', then 'what you do in such a position' (i.e. teach), and then, later still, 'the communication made and recorded under such circumstances'; and because the latter is confidential, finally the word comes to mean 'a piece of secret, esoteric teaching'.

C. F. Andrews held that the remarkably fertile imagination disclosed in the Upanishads was produced chiefly by a later migration of the Nordic race, which had settled farther down country on the borders of Nepal. These colonists appear to have come originally without their families, and to have taken wives from among the inhabitants, and it may be that the mixture of race produced new types of mental activity.

There were probably at one time more than 300 Upanishads in existence, but Narayana's collection (c. A.D. 1400) contained only fifty-two, and Prince Dara Shukoh's collection, translated into Persian (1656-7), contained sixty. This Persian edition was rendered into Latin in 1801 by a French scholar, Anquetil du Perron (1723-1805), who brought it home to Paris together with a copy of the Zendavests and some 180 other MSS. Thus in the first decade of the nineteenth century Europe became acquainted with these extraordinary compositions, but, be it noted, in a translation made from a translation. It is probable that this rather isolated study led to the value of the documents being a trifle over-estimated, since there was then no knowledge of their context, or of the circumstances of their composition.

A late list of Upanishads gives the number as 108. It appears, however, that the great majority of these are of relatively recent date, and sectarian in character. Of the really old ones only a few dozen survive, and of these the principal are fourteen in number. Of these, six are in archaic prose. This might seem to give some clue as to dating, and if the classification be accepted, the following results are reached—

the names given being the titles by which these Upanishads are generally known.

		Usually accepted orders of date	Orders as arranged by Oldenburg and Keith
Six early prose almost unanimously accepted as the oldest	Aitareya	3	1
	Kaushitaki	5	4
	Chandogya	2	3
	Kena	6	6
	Taittiriya	4	5
	Brhadaranyaka	1	2
Five metrical	Katha		
	Svetasvatara		
	Mahanarayana		
	Isa		
	Mundaka		
Three later prose	Maitri		
	Prasna		
	Mandukya		

Professor Belvalkar, however, in 1925 published a totally different analysis of the documents. He considers that even the existing Upanishads are composite, and that they contain matter of varying dates. By applying stylometric tests, and considering cross-quotations and ideological developments, he has finally reached a new classification in four divisions, which Rawson summarises as follows:[4]

GROUP I	GROUP II	GROUP III (a)
Ait. ii, 1—3	Isa	Katha I, i, ii.
Br. i, 1—3	Baskala	Ch. v, 3—10
Ch. i, ii.	Ait.	Br. vi, 2
Ait. iii	Br. i, 4—6	Kaus i.
Tait. i.	vi, 1—3	Katha, I, iii
Kena iii, iv.	Ch. iii,	Mund.
	iv, 16—17	Svet i.
	v, 1—2	Prasna
	Tait. ii, 1—5, 9	Ch. iv, v, 11—24
	iii, 1—6	vi.
	Kena i, ii.	Br. ii, 1, 4, iii
	Chaqaleya	iv, 2
		Arseya

4 *Katha Upanished*, p. 9 in the Introduction.

GROUP III (b)	GROUP IV
Katha II	Ch. vii,
Tait. ii, 6—8	viii, 13—15
iii, 7—10	Br. v, vi, 4.
Ch. viii, 1—12	Svet. ii, iii, iv.
Br. ii, 2, 3, 5	Mand.
iv, 3—5	Mait. iii.—vii.
Kaus ii, iii, iv.	
Svet. v, vi.	
Mait. i, ii.	

The above scheme is given, not as a final analysis of the literature in question, but for the convenience of any student who may wish to try a course of reading in the texts themselves.

Various opinions have been expressed as to the course of the development of the doctrines which are found in the Upanishads. Deussen holds that the idealistic monism of Yajñavalkya which occurs in the Brhadaranyaka Up. is the main doctrine which was first definitely taught. Berriedale Keith dissents from this, and holds that Yajñavalkya is an advanced and profound but strongly individualised interpreter of doctrine, who did not succeed in winning acceptance for some generations, and that he stands aside from the main stream of Upanishadic thought. Belvalkar thinks that Upanishadic idealism may have come towards the end of the whole process; while Deussen considers that the doctrine 'begins with a bold and blunt idealism, and from thence by an accommodation to popular thought through the phases of pantheism, cosmogonism, and theism, reacting eventually to the atheism of the later Sāmkhya, and the apsychism of early Buddhism'.

Since dating and textual criticism involve a large subjective element on the part of critics, it seems best to take the Upanishads as a whole, just as they have come to us and have been commented upon.

Each Upanishad was (at first) orally transmitted as the record of a particular school or group of disciples. Hence it contained all kinds of miscellaneous matters which it was thought desirable to preserve as part of tradition. This explains the occurrence of the same material in more than one Upanishad. Favourite passages were memorised and used for meditation in more than one locality. Thus in the Brhadaranyaka Up. are to be found stanzas identical with some which occur also in the Isa and the Katha Ups., while in the Svetasvatara are passages which can be paralleled in the Katha and the Mundaka. The Maitri again has stanzas which occur in the Taittiriya, and so on. This is partly due to the fact that all the various teachers were commenting upon and interpreting the same Vedic literature. Hence they tend to

D

give the same verse quotations. But by far the largest part of the Upanishadic material consists of memorised reminiscences of teachers and their doctrine. Sometimes the *vamsa* or line of tradition (a kind of apostolic succession) is laboriously recorded, as in the 6th Brahmana of the Brhadaranyaka. At other times a verbatim account of a conversation is given, or a list of short sayings, not at all unlike the 'Pirke Aboth' or 'Sayings of the Fathers', of Rabbinical Judaism. Or it may be that an exposition is given of primitive physics. Interspersed between all these items are ejaculatory prayers (e.g., those to be used before marital relations); ceremonial instructions, occasional offices, e.g., prayers at the new moon, or on the return of a father to his family; and even prescriptions for a love-potion and for procuring a specially desired object. Some of these latter are obviously excrescences on the main stem of the literature.

There are, however, a number of leading ideas which stand out as characteristic of the Upanishadic corpus of documents. True it contains no system, and no one single philosophy—since commentators have found in it support for their own preferences, and have deduced, from the various texts, pantheistic, theistic and even atheistic conclusions. Nevertheless, the most frequently reiterated doctrine is that of the One Atman. The spirit of the inquiry is nowhere more frankly displayed than in the opening sentences of the Svetasvatara:

> 'What is the cause?—Brahma?—Whence are we born?—
> Whereby do we live?—And on what are we established?—
> Over-ruled by Whom, in pains and pleasures,
> Do we live our various conditions, O ye theologians?—'[5]

and the chief answer, recurring at intervals, is nowhere more clearly stated than in the Chandogya:

> 'Verily this whole world is Brahma. Tranquil let him worship It as That from which he came forth, as That into Which he will be dissolved, as That in Which he breathes.'[6]

On the other hand, the Aitareya shows in its first stanza that some sages were still thinking in terms of a Creator-God:

> 'In the beginning Atman (the Great Self or Soul) was here, one only; no other thing that openeth the eye. He bethought Himself: Let me now

5 Hume. *The Thirteen Principal Upanishads*, p. 394.
6 Hume, op. cit. p. 209.

create worlds. . . . He bethought Himself: Here now are worlds. Let me now create world-guardians, etc., etc.'[7]

The similarity of this to Genesis i will be apparent. Yet by the end of the Aitareya we find ourselves back at the conception of the One Atman Who is Everything, i.e., Brahma, Indra, all the gods, the five elements, things born from an egg or from a womb, whatever organic life there is, moving or stationary, and so on. This is complete non-duality, or, as it is called in India, *advaita*, and the realisation of it is held to be the knowledge which completely liberates. Such knowledge, however, is not to be won lightly, but only by austerity, by the practice of self-control, and by the negating of all the passions. One Upanishad, the Mundaka, goes so far as to declare that it is not even obtainable by one's own efforts, but only by revelation granted to whomsoever the Great Self chooses to reveal it. The result is complete union with the Absolute:

> 'As the flowing rivers in the ocean
> Disappear, quitting name and form,
> So the knower, being liberated from name and form,
> Goes unto the Heavenly Person, higher than the high.'[8]

and again:

'He, verily, who knows that Supreme Brahma, becomes very Brahma. He crosses over sorrow and sin. Liberated from the knots of the heart he becomes immortal.'[9] Anquetil du Perron rendered this in a Latin translation or rather paraphrase, and set it at the head of his version, thus: *Quisquis Deum intelligit, Deus fit.* Put in this western dress, the doctrine is clear. Whatever its merits or demerits, it is completely distinct from the doctrine of the Christian mystics as such, since, although they sometimes in rhapsody approach very near to it (and the more so when under the influence of the quasi-Christian writer pseudo-Dionysius), even Eckhart says somewhere that in the height of ecstasy, when God and the soul seem most closely united: 'God stays God and soul stays soul.'[10]

and this separateness is affirmed by a modern Jesuit scholar, Fr. Erich Przywara,[11] in his Catholic philosophy of religion. A similar doctrine

7 Hume, op. cit. p. 294.
8 Hume, op. cit. p. 376.
9 Hume, op. cit. p. 377.
10 Eckhart, 41st Sermon, 2nd series. But see article by the author in *Theology*, April 1940, for a full discussion of the point.
11 Eng. trans. 'Polarity'. pp. 119 ff.

came later to be held by a minority group of Hindu thinkers, and is called *vishistadvaita*, or modified non-duality (qualified monism). But the majority-belief is simply that expressed in the Mandukya Upanishad: 'Truly everything here is Brahma; this self is Brahma. Even this very self has four fourths'[12] (i.e., the whole of it is Brahma).

Certain items are often taken for granted as axiomatic and form a background to this doctrine.

First, all empiric existence as such is an evil thing.

Second, all such empiric existence involves an infinite series of never-ending births and deaths. This chain of finite existences is called *samsara*, and the circumstances under which the individual is re-born are determined by his *karma* (lit. action), i.e., the effect of his deeds, from which there is no escape.

Third, deliverance from this cycle is desirable, and is of the nature of 'salvation' (*moksha* or release).

Fourth, such deliverance or salvation is to be obtained primarily by knowledge of the Supreme Truth about Brahma-Atman, which gives the possessor of it power over his own destiny. The soul is conceived as a pilgrim, and its final goal is the 'waning out' (*nirvana*) of desire, or of what the modern psychologist calls *libido*.

Fifth. Ascetic discipline and frugal chastity are necessary preliminaries to the attainment of a state of consciousness in which such knowledge is possible.

It is obvious that unless these axioms are agreed upon, the way of the Upanishadic teachers is not acceptable. The problem that interests us is why so many did accept it. Can we point to any fundamental development in Indian thought which might have caused this apparent departure from the hearty genial piety of the earlier portions of the Rig-Veda and the adoption of the rather sombre pessimism of the Upanishadic age?

Perhaps the answer might be that the cause of the change was precisely this axiomatic background, comprising the development of the ideas of transmigration and of escape from *samsara*. It would seem as though these ideas, absent from the Rig-Veda, appeared early in the Upanishadic age as a theory of cosmic life, rather in the way that the idea of evolution developed in Western Europe during the nineteenth century after Christ. At first they were seen to be so sinister that those who adopted them as a working theory were almost afraid of their effect upon the public. 'Take my hand, my friend,' says Yajñavalkya: 'we two alone shall know of this. Let this question of ours be not

12 Hume, op. cit. p. 391.

discussed openly.' So he and his colleague go out, and debate *in camera* the effects of *karma*, i.e., action as determining the condition under which one is re-born. But the truth as they conceived it could not be hid, and whether we of the twentieth century agree with it or not, the world of India accepted it as a melancholy but indisputable discovery, and from that time onward, Hindu philosophical theology is based upon it, and by it the endeavours of the earnestly pious are conditioned.

A distinguished modern Hindu (Mr. V. Krishnaswami Iyev) has asserted that he cannot imagine any follower of Hinduism who is not a believer in *karma* and transmigration. With this assumed, it is small wonder that the Hindu world-view has tended to become pessimistic.

It is possible that we may not be wise to read the original Upanishadic records in the light of what later commentators have written about them. It may be that the original Upanishadic schools were not so much infected with world-negation and pessimism as with a restless search for Divine truth, and that they were therefore realistic in facing the facts of life, which plainly include a large measure of impermanence and the inevitability of physical death. It cannot, however, be denied that India for many generations has not only set the question of man's spiritual perfection and the problem of his spiritual future at the centre of all thought, but has also answered it generally in one specific way. Europeans and Americans, and, perhaps especially, British and modern Russians, are so much occupied with their activity *in the world* that they give less heed to the ultimate questions.

The next leading ideas which we find throughout the Upanishads are (1) negatively, the abandonment or the supersession of objective sacrifice, and (2) positively, the doctrine that knowledge can take its place. This pair of propositions constitutes, as will be seen, something in the nature of a spiritual revolution. Such a revolution probably sprang less from the priestly section of the community than from the lay and warrior section, from the Kshatriyas rather than from the Brahmins. Indeed it may well have begun as a kind of protest against the monopoly of religion by the priestly caste. The latter, as we have seen, expected high fees for the performance of the ceremonial rites, but such rites, it must be remembered, were widely believed to be necessary for the physical well-being of the community, much as are the offices of physicians and surgeons today. Any attempt at short-circuiting these rites would therefore amount to a situation in modern society in which ordinary lay-folk said to one another: 'The medical profession are charging too much for curing us. We will start our own lay movement of preventive medicine and hygiene, and so cut out

the necessity of employing these very expensive professional prac-
titioners.' This, of course, is not an exact parallel, but it may give some
idea of the sort of thing that began to occur. Thus we read (Mundaka
1, 2, 7 and 10):

> 'Unsafe boats . . . are these sacrificial forms.
> Thinking sacrifice and merit is the chiefest thing,
> Naught better do they know—deluded.'[13]

and the teaching which follows is to the effect that uncontentious, un-
obtrusive ascetics who aim at knowledge attain to unity with the
Absolute Reality without any sacrifice at all. Again (Chandogya 8.5)
we learn that the true equivalent of what is commonly called sacrifice
(*yajña*) or the sacrificial victim (*ista*) or a protracted sacrifice (*sattrayana*)
is really the chaste life of the student of knowledge.

As Hume sums it up: 'The whole religious doctrine of the gods and
of the necessity of sacrificing to them is seen to be a stupendous fraud,
by the man who has acquired metaphysical knowledge of the monistic
unity of self and the world in Brahma or Atman'[14] (—the One Great
Absolute Being Who is beyond personality).

Rawson, commenting on the Katha Upanishad, goes so far as to
say that this doctrine is proclaimed again and again by the Upanishadic
teachers not as mere metaphysical speculation, but as actually a liberating gospel.[15] The idea of sacrifice is, in fact, either re-interpreted or
abandoned altogether. Either the old rites are given new meaning or
enlarged, or else the enlightened believer passes beyond them and
finds salvation in knowledge. This idea of a special kind of knowledge
as affecting the liberation of the soul is perhaps one of the most distinctive features of higher Indian religion; but it is important to avoid
any misunderstanding as to what it involves. The knowledge which
so liberates is not the sort of knowledge that the Western world of
today derives from empirical science, and values so highly. There
are those, for example, who have found the works of Eddington or of
Russell, with their synthetic accounts of the nature of the physical
universe derived from observation and experiment, to be extremely
liberating; but the Indian philosophers of the Upanishadic age did not
mean this kind of thing. Theirs was partly the fruit of an introspection
even more drastic than that of Descartes, partly the result of a technique
which aimed at inducing abnormal states of consciousness. Salvation

13 Hume, op. cit. p. 368.
14 Hume, op. cit. p. 53.
15 Rawson, op. cit. p. 34.

through knowledge (*vidya*) is thus much more of the same type as that known in the Hellenistic world of the second century A.D. as γνῶσις. Indeed, one of the discourses attributed to Hermes Trismegistos is remarkably like an Upanishad, and the effect produced on the disciple by his instructor is to make him exclaim ecstatically that '*now* he sees himself in mind'—i.e., as he really is, in his true nature. The solitary ascetic teachers of the forest schools, some of whom are mentioned by name (Yajñavalkya, Balaki, Sanatkunara, Pippalada) as being resorted to by inquirers, gave not only intellectual instruction, but also advice on the technique of controlling the breath and the limbs as well as the inner mind, so as to induce a state of quiescence in which supreme awareness of Reality might be attained. Sometimes a Upanishad will give a long list of the succession of teachers in a particular spot, and from these it is clear that a school of wisdom (such as in later Hinduism is called an *ashrama*) often became established, and that persons resorted to it for a kind of higher education, and often remained for some considerable time, practising spiritual exercises and austere discipline.

Out of these schools there ultimately emerged certain more or less well-defined types of doctrine and practice. It is usual to say that India has had six great systems of philosophy, and in the next chapter we shall describe some of these; but the great ideas which have just been described are probably the dominating ones in the literature under consideration. There is no reason for supposing that they immediately penetrated far into the minds of the masses of the population everywhere. Actually they were only the sophisticated teachings of a minority and even perhaps rather a class affair. The old practices of sacrifice have endured to this very day among large sections of the orthodox Hindu population, and in the eighteenth century the Abbé Dubois found them as prevalent as ever, though since his time European education and Christian influence have undermined them to some extent. What has happened, however, is that the Hinduism of the Brahmins has adopted the new teaching into itself, and has created a *modus vivendi* for it side by side with the older ceremonial, by framing the tolerant doctrine of the various kinds of *yoga* or spiritual exercises.

To *yoga* we shall return in detail in a later chapter. Here it is enough to remark that the way of knowledge is called Jñana Yoga, the ways of physical and spiritual exercise are Hatha Yoga and Raja Yoga, while the way of ceremonial or works is called Karma Yoga. Even in the Upanishads themselves there are passages in which ceremonial sacrifice is still recognised. The same apparent inconsistency can be found in Hebrew literature, where at one time all sacrifice is swept aside as superfluous and futile (as in Micah vi), while at another it is retained, side by side with the higher doctrine (as in Psalm li, where we read: 'The sacrifices of God are a broken spirit,' and in the next verse but one: 'then shall they offer young bullocks upon Thine altar').

The truth would seem to be that the human spirit in religious matters is extremely conservative, and is loth to abandon any practice which in the past has seemed religiously profitable. In any case there is always the sub-conscious fear: 'What will happen to me or the world if we stop performing the ancient sacrifices?' So in the end there is almost always a compromise. Mohammed goes to Mecca as an iconoclast, but ends by allowing a good many of the old Kaaba ceremonies to go on, and there they are to this day. The Hebrew prophets and Christ taught the abandonment of ritual sacrifice, but although early Christian writings contain a number of passages of a most radical nature, after about the time of the Cappadocian Fathers in the fourth century, ritual sacrifice creeps back in a variety of forms, and even persists in Catholic circles to the present time, though, it is true, highly spiritualised.

It is rather difficult to give the feeling of the Upanishadic 'gospel', without using some sort of illustration, and the reader must not take what follows too literally; but if we use our imagination we can picture the situation as analogous to what might happen were Mr. Bernard Shaw's *Life-Force* or the Marx-Leninist *Dialectic Process* proclaimed as aspects of the one and only Absolute Deity. Thus one great Upanishadic seer, Yajñavalkya, when asked by a disciple, Sakalya, how many gods there are, first gives a traditional answer, thirty-three great gods and 3,306 devas or lesser deities. But when pressed, he reduces the number successively to six, three, two, one-and-half, and finally to one—whom he calls *Prana*, which means 'Life Power' or 'Breath of Life', as the Greeks might say: *Pneuma;* or a modern Frenchman, *L'élan vital*.

Whether world-and-life-negation and the quest for union with this One Supreme Power was induced by some debilitating factor in the climate of India is doubtful. It is, of course, possible that Dravidians and pre-Dravidians were more easily able to acclimatise than the Nordics from the Asiatic plateau lands, but Sir Charles Eliot declares that he did not find the climate of India unpleasant, taken as a whole, provided that one got adjusted to it. Moreover, it is quite evident that plenty of the inhabitants of India have been both active, industrious, and life-affirming. In earlier times, as Nehru reminds us, Indians were lacking neither in mental alertness nor in technical skill. The words of

Eliot are worth quoting as the verdict of an enlightened Englishman:[16]

'In Eastern Asia the influence of India has been notable in extent, strength and duration. Scant justice is done to her position in the world by those histories which recount the exploits of her invaders, and leave the impression that her own people were a feeble, dreamy folk, sundered from the rest of mankind by their sea and mountain frontiers. Such a picture takes no account of the intellectual conquests of the Hindus. Even their political conquests were not contemptible and were remarkable for the distance if not for the extent of the territory occupied. For there were Hindu kingdoms in Java and Camboja and settlements in Sumatra and even in Borneo, an island about as far from India as Persia is from Rome. But such military or commercial achievements are insignificant compared with the spread of Indian thought. The south-eastern region of Asia—both mainland and archipelago—owed its civilisation almost entirely to India. In Ceylon, Burma, Siam, Camboja, Champa, and Java, religion, art, the alphabet, literature, as well as whatever science and political organisation existed, were the direct gifts of Hindus, whether Brahmins or Buddhists, and much the same may be said of Tibet, whence the wilder Mongols took as much Indian civilisation as they could stomach.'

Nehru's opinion is that the ideology of the Upanishads did not permeate to any marked extent the masses of Indians, but that for reasons which it is now difficult to determine there were from about A.D. 1000 signs of inner decay in Indian civilisation. Her people grew tired, and long before the advent of European invaders she was in a state of deterioration and decline. 'Indian life became a sluggish stream, living in the past, moving slowly through the accumulations of the centuries.'[17] The use and interpretation of the Upanishads during the last 900 years may not represent their original trend. They may have fallen into the hands of those who, like the Greeks of late antiquity, had come to feel deep misgivings about the world, and had lost their nerve in facing it, and who thus, instead of devoting themselves to activity, were more concerned with redemption out of the world.

However this may be, it is certain that the centuries which saw the rise and development of the Upanishadic schools were times of intense intellectual and spiritual ferment, and it is certain also that only fragmentary records of them have been preserved and transmitted to later generations. Of some important movements which emerged from the midst of this ferment we must speak in the next chapter.

16 Eliot, op. cit. vol. i, p. 12.
17 Nehru, op. cit. ch. xxi.

A brief survey of some of the leading features in the principal Upanishads may be worth setting forth.[18]

In the Kena, which is one of the shorter ones, we find declared the doctrine of the prevenience of Brahma, who, though inscrutable, precedes and conditions all that is; and the quasi-Barthian paradox is stated:

> It is conceived of by him by whom It is not conceived of;
> He by whom It is conceived of knows it not.

In the Katha the Divine Reality is described as invisible, all-pervading, yet hidden deep, and only to be realised through the spiritual touch. This is a longer Upanishad, and it is one of the most interesting and most popular. The conclusion to which it seems to come is that the Inward Reality cannot be fathomed by philosophical reasoning, but only by mystical experience.

The Prasna, which is of moderate length, is largely concerned with an attempted psychological analysis of human personality, which it represents as separable into sixteen elements. It contains a hymn in praise of the Life-Force.

The Mundaka opens with a dialogue concerning the theory of knowledge, and here is encountered that special hostility to the sacrificial system, which has been mentioned and which is here stigmatised as the occupation of fools. The knowledge of the Divine Reality is to be sought not through ritual but through instruction accompanied by self-discipline.

The Mandukya, another small Upanishad, describes the approximation of the finite self to the Great Self through four stages: first, the waking stage; second, the dream stage; third, dreamless sleep; and fourth, complete identification, wherein all appearances and all duality have ceased. The negative teaching of this Upanishad reminds one strongly of the subsequent nihilistic doctrines of monastic Buddhism. Here we learn that the Divine Reality is unperceived, unrelated to experience, unknowable, unthinkable, unnameable, indefinable, the One in which everything else has ceased.

In the Taittirya the chief emphasis is upon the casting out of all fear by the realisation that the nature of Brahman is pure bliss (*ananda*), unthinkable by the mind, and unutterable in speech.

The very long Chandogya expounds by many devices (including the famous parable of the salt in the water) the doctrine that the

18 I am indebted for advice about this section to Professor S. N. Dasgupta.

entire Universe is the Divine Essence, which is nothing but the highest
Self, differentiated though It may be into a multiplicity of entities
endowed with 'name and form'.

The Brhadaranyaka, also very long, makes the notable contribution
that the Essential Self is to be loved beyond all else in the world, and
proceeds to emphasise the necessity of perceiving that duality is an
illusion, so that 'holding the Self as dear' is not an I-Thou relationship,
but an identification which is of the quality of pure bliss. Similarly all
beings in the world are to be loved, and all beings experience this
bliss, solely because they are all grounded in the Great Self as their
Final Cause. It is not a far cry from this to the essential teaching of the
Buddha.

In some of the Upanishads the Brahman is the Lord, or Transcendent
Reality, controlling the Universe as it were externally. In others the
Brahman is as definitely the Inward Essence of Man. There is no one
consistent theology. The different possible types of religious experience
are all emphasised in turn, but how the 'many' making up the
Universe can arise out of the 'One' or Great Self, or in what sense
the reality of the world can be regarded as spiritually grounded, is
not explained.

The Isa Upanishad, often selected by the student for first reading
because of its extreme brevity, is actually one of the hardest and
most profound. It contains passages repeated elsewhere, but its main
theme is that everything has to be surrendered to the Great Self, who
is styled Isa or Lord—an unusually personal title for this literature.

Perhaps the best way to sum up is to say, in the words of a modern
Hindu philosopher, that the whole atmosphere of the Upanishads
seems to be ringing with mystical music, and that the sages were
almost intoxicated with their discovery of the Highest Reality or
Innermost Self of man, and with the discovery that everything we
perceive around us is Brahman, so that all our thoughts, all our being
all our experience are grounded in the Latter, and that in spite of
apparent diversities there is only the One Ultimate Reality in which
both the microcosm and the macrocosm are united.

The full extent of the influence of all this Indian religious and philosophical activity upon the world of Hellas we shall perhaps never be
in a position to estimate, but it seems certain that it had its effect upon
the thinkers of Ionia, since in the time of Alexander the Great the
court physician Hecataeus travelled as far as the Punjab, and there is
no reason for doubting that at an earlier date trade routes were open
between India and the Mediterranean, so that intellectual as well as

material commerce may have flowed along them, It would appear that some sort of Indian ascetic appeared at Athens in the days of Plato, and Plato's Parmenides is held to show traces of Upanishadic thought.

It is significant that the school of Cynic philosophers was founded somewhere about the time of Alexander's invasion of India. Diogenes, who originated it, decided to live in the most austere and primitive manner—'like a dog'. Hence the name *kunikos*, or 'dog-like'. He subsisted by begging, after the manner of an Indian *sadhu*, and claimed fellowship not only with all human beings but with animals as well.[19]

We will conclude here with a striking passage from the early Chandogya Upanishad. In this, its seventh great section, the disciple Narada comes to his teacher Sanatkumara and asks for instruction, saying in effect, I have memorised all the ordinary Vedic literature—what lack I yet? One thing I lack—peace of mind. 'It has been heard by me from those who are like you, sir, that he who knows the Soul (Atman) crosses over sorrow. Such a sorrowing one am I, sir. Do you cause me, who am such a one, to cross over to the other side of sorrow.'[20] Sanatkumara in reply takes Narada through twenty-six lessons or Khandas, in each of which there is an ascent from the mere text of the Vedas, i.e., Name (or as we should say, 'words'). This ascent goes from Name to Speech, from Speech to Mind, from Mind to Conception, from Conception to Thought, from Thought to Meditation, from Meditation to Understanding, from Understanding to Strength, from Strength to Food, from Food to Water, from Water to Heat, from Heat to Space, from Space to Memory, from Memory to Hope, from Hope to Life or Breath (Prana), and finally the answer is given from a Vedic verse:

> The seer sees not death,
> Nor sickness nor any distress,
> The seer sees only the All,
> Obtains the All entirely.[21]

Liberation is found, in fact, by a mental discipline, in which one traces everything back to its Ultimate Source. Here, it is implied, is peace, and the banishment of the sorrow which comes from the sense of impermanence or evanescence.

19 *See* Bertrand Russell, *History of Western Philosophy*, p. 254.
20 Hume, op. cit. pp. 250 ff.
21 Hume, op. cit. p. 262.

BOOKS FOR FURTHER STUDY

PROFESSOR BERRIEDALE KEITH. Op. cit.

PROFESSOR S. N. DASGUPTA. *History of Indian Philosophy*. Cambridge. 1922. *Indian Idealism*. Cambridge. 1933.

PROFESSOR R. E. HUME. *The Thirteen Principal Upanishads*. Oxford. 1931.

J. N. RAWSON. *The Katha Upanishad*. Oxford. 1934.

4

THE GREAT MOVEMENTS
JAINISM AND BUDDHISM

As time went on, philosophical and religious thought in India began
to crystallise into more or less distinct groups. There are usually said to
have been six of them: (1) Nyaya; (2) Vaishesika; (3) Sāmkhya;
(4) Yoga; (5) Purva Mimamsa; (6) Uttara Mimamsa or Vedānta.
Nyaya is a kind of Hindu scholasticism, full of close analytic reasoning,
and contains a belief in a personal God, in finite souls and in an atomic
universe. The Vaishesika is somewhat similar, but lays stress upon the
separateness of individual selves and objects. According to European
standards (4) and (5) are not, strictly speaking, philosophies at all,
Yoga being an elaborate spiritual technique for producing exalted
states of consciousness, and Purva Mimamsa a polytheistic ritualism,
based upon a rather slavish use of logic. It is Sāmkhya and Vedānta
which constitute the really important philosophical systems. Of these,
the Sāmkhya, though commonly described as dualistic, because of its
two 'primary causes', *prakrti* or matter and *purushas* or finite selves, is
really pluralistic, since the number of *purushas* is infinite and persisting.
They are, in fact, almost exactly like the 'primary parts' of Dr.
McTaggart's famous system. The Vedanta, on the contrary, is through
and through monistic, and in its later or medieval shape, when
developed by the great teacher Sankara, it became the outstanding
example of a system built upon the principle of *advaita* or non-duality.
As such it is the logical outcome of a concentration upon those passages
in the Upanishads which speak of the One Atman.

*   *   *   *   *

Long before these philosophical systems were complete, though not before the development of the two lines of thought typified by the Sāmkhya and the Vedānta, and in the very midst of all the ferment, we see two special movements taking shape in North India. One of these, Jainism, has always been small in size though not in influence, and has never extended itself outside India, though its members may have been known to the outside world as gymnosophists, for reasons which will shortly appear. The other, Buddhism, has been one of the most potent spiritual forces in the whole of Asia. In this volume no attempt can be made to describe either of these movements in detail, and certainly not to recount the expansion of Buddhism outside India; yet as episodes in the history of Hinduism, the origin and rise of both Jainism and Buddhism must certainly be considered. Buddhism is described in detail in a separate volume in this series.

We may picture the young men of good social standing at this period going from one teacher to another to learn culture and sharpen their intellects. The structure of the Upanishads shows this; and it is clear that the Upanishadic schools played somewhat the part of the modern University college, or of a medieval monastery, in providing a kind of higher education. The core of such communities consisted of a few 'fully professed' individuals, who were engaged in practising a severely disciplined and abstemious life, the chief aim being to acquire extreme bodily self-control, and by certain exercises (*tāpas*) to reach an exalted state of consciousness. Who first invented such exercises we do not know. They may have been developed as far back as the days of the proto-Dravidian civilisation, or even earlier. In many parts of the world, some form of alcohol or other drug has been regarded as possessing supernatural properties, and has been used by Shamans or medicine men for the purpose of inducing special states of ecstasy. Thus among some tribes of American Indians the root *peyote* is used in this way as well as for medical purposes, and among Moslem devotees musical instruments are also employed for helping meditation. It is thought that the Brahmin priesthood, who were, so to speak, super-Shamans, came to discover how to induce ecstasy first of all by the use of the sacred alcohol, *soma*, and then later by fasting, mortification of the flesh, and auto-hypnotic processes. But at the time of which we speak here, the attempt at the practice of such ascetic exercises was being made not merely by the priestly caste, but by the Kshatriya or warrior caste as well, perhaps with the idea of breaking down a Brahmin monopoly.

I JAINISM

One such attempt is associated with a Kshatriya called Vardhamana (*c.* 599 to 529 B.C.), though he hardly seems to have been its founder, but rather the author of a successful revival of a movement which had begun some 250 years earlier. Of the real founder, Parsva, almost nothing is known, but he may well have been an extreme ascetic, since the parents of Vardhamana are said to have been disciples of his sect, and they, when their son was thirty-one years of age, decided to engage in a 'fast unto death', a practice which has been characteristic of Jain zealots. After the voluntary decease of his father and mother. Vardhamana renounced the world and the wearing of clothes, and wandered about in Bengal like Solomon Eagle in the City of London in the reign of Charles II, performing austerities and enduring persecutions. After thirteen years of this, he declared that he had gained enlightenment or *samadhi*, and became the head of a group of devotees, calling himself Jina or Jaina (i.e., one who has attained freedom from bondage—'the victorious one'). His followers referred to him not by his personal name but as *Mahavira*, which means 'the great hero' (rather as Italians would have spoken of 'the Duce'). The Jain community still exists, and numbers roughly about a million and a half adherents. Jains are keen educationalists and are also successful in business. The standard of literacy among them is high, and their moral code elevated. They tend to amass fortunes which they spent until recently on elegant temples, but now employ more on building and maintaining schools, and also hospitals for sick animals.

From the time of Mahavira onwards, Jains have displayed certain specific features, and have developed doctrines of a rather peculiar and distinctive character, which may well go back to the days of the founder and which have exercised an influence on the main stream of Hinduism. It seems fairly clear that Vardhamana's intellectual background was that of the Sāmkhya philosophy in its atheistic form. Thus Jains usually deny the existence of a Supreme Being, and treat the Absolute as consisting of a plurality of souls. The world is eternal and self-existent, and is made up of six constituent elements, units of matter, space, time, certain forces called *dharma* and *adharma*, and souls. They venerate a number of saintly leaders called Tirthankara, all of whom are declared to have belonged to the Kshatriya caste (another hit at the Brahmins). The aim of individual souls is by strict self-discipline to attain to the condition called Jiva or bliss, and so to become oneself a Jina, or conqueror. There is a distinction between monks and nuns on the one hand, and laity on the other. Monks and nuns have to follow a stringent rule of life. The laity are bound by minor vows, and are committed to the revering and maintenance of the ascetics. Very extreme mortification is practised, and one division of the Jain community eschews entirely the wearing of clothes. Others who wear garments must not kill vermin which may lodge in them, nor, if they are meditating, must they move in order to scratch themselves.

Great reverence for all forms of organic life is taught, under the name of *ahimsa* (literally harmlessness), and Hindus like Gandhi have developed this idea so as to include pacifism and non-violent passive resistance. Jains themselves carry *ahimsa* to its logical conclusion in such practices as sweeping the ground before them as they walk, in order to avoid treading on living creatures, straining their drinks, screening their lamps from insects, and even wearing respirators so as to avoid breathing in micro-organisms. They observe great kindness to animals, and maintain asylums for sick beasts. They prohibit both the sacrifice of animals and their slaughter for food, and even collect and rear young ones which their owners have discarded as superfluous (thus they would say that instead of drowning surplus kittens we ought to send them without exception to a cats' home). Five vows have to be taken by a fully professed Jain: (1) not to kill; (2) not to speak untruths; (3) to take nothing that is not given; (4) to observe chastity; (5) to renounce all pleasures in external objects. Rule (1) includes all speech or thought which might bring about a quarrel and so provoke a crime of violence, and self-discipline is not merely external, but includes mental exercises, acts of humiliation, and so on. The fast unto death is still in theory observable, provided one has first undergone twelve years' penance. Jain temples are clean and brightly coloured, and are visited daily by the laity, chiefly for the purpose of venerating the Tirthankaras, whose images are to be seen all around in their respective chapels. It used to be an act of great merit to increase the number of temples and shrines. The worship consists chiefly in the offering of flowers, incense, and lights, accompanied by the singing of hymns in prase of the Jain saints.

Three points may be stressed in conclusion:

(1) The moral precept of *ahimsa* (pronounced *ahingsa*) or harmlessness has developed in modern Hinduism into one of positive kindness, or rather perhaps the daily practice of what has been called the silver rule (the negative form of the golden rule).

(2) Jainism is probably the antecedent, if not the parent, of

E

Buddhism. The founder of the latter movement may have been for a time a visitor to a Jain community.

(3) Jainism in the past fifty years has produced a noted saint, Vijaya Dharma Suri, who, in a sermon preached before the Maharaja of Benares, taught that it was an error to call the Jains atheists, since they accepted the belief in Paramatman, the Self-Existent Being. It does not appear that his point of view represents that of the majority of Jains. Literature supplied to the author from their official publishing centre is entirely non-committal as to the existence of any deity, and is chiefly concerned with ethics.

II BUDDHISM

Siddhartha Gautama of the Sakya clan was, like Vardhamana, a scion of the Kshatriya caste, and his father was of the status of a local chieftain, though it is possible that he may have held an elective and temporary office rather than a permanent and hereditary title. The territory of the clan lay on the border which now runs between Nepal and the United Provinces. Its chief town was Kapilavasthu, probably about 150 miles north of Benares, and the reputed site of the house where Gautama was born, in the Lumbini Park, is marked by a pillar. The name Gautama is a family or surname, and other Gautamas are mentioned in Indian literature (e.g., in the first Adhya of the Kaushitaki Up.). Hence this particular individual is usually referred to by some honorific titles such as *buddha*, the Enlightened One, *tathagata*, He who conforms to a standard type, or simply *bhagava*, Lord. He grew up as a Hindu, just at the time when the Upanishadic movement had borne its fruits. There seems no doubt that he married in the normal fashion, and begat a son. There seems also no doubt that for some deep reason connected with the urge to discover a way of liberation of spirit for himself and others, he left home on a wandering or pilgrimage, doubtless with every intention of coming back again. There are various chronicles of his journey, and one of the places where he is said to have stayed is Vesali, to which in later life he seems to have been much attached, and with which, from his earliest adventures, he had strong associations. Now it is known that close to Vesali there was an important Jain settlement, and Gautama's early experiments in asceticism seem to indicate that he knew the Jain movement, and had even been a member of it, at any rate for a time. It is also clear that Gautama's intellectual background was that of the older Upanishads. His language, and the very terms he uses, show this, even though he diverges from the ordinary line of Hindu thought.

Both Jainism and Buddhism tend to break away from the caste system, and if it is true that Jainism seems to show an affinity with the Sāmkhya philosophy, early Buddhism would seem equally to have affinities with both Sāmkhya and Vedānta. A certain amount of misunderstanding has ensued from earlier students of Buddhism having treated it without due regard for this background. Thus the word *atta* in Buddhist literature has been read as though it meant merely a finite self, whereas Gautama in one of his earliest sayings speaks like Prajapati in the Chandogya Up. of the *Great Self* as 'that which is to be searched out'. When, on his death-bed, Gautama tells his disciples to be *attadipa*, he does not mean that they are to be those who are lamps unto themselves, but as those who have the Self for a lamp. It seems clear, however, that Gautama's mysticism was an extreme instance of the identity-type, in which subject and object are fused to such an extent that Deity, so to speak, becomes a subjective state of consciousness, or, as Dr. Inge once put it, 'an atmosphere rather than an object'. This is really only a short step beyond the *advaita* or non-duality doctrine of the Hindu monist 'That art thou' or 'I am It'. Once Brahma is divested of the ordinary attributes of personality and identified with the finite self, it is not a far cry to the strict Buddhist position of agnosticism over the question whether there is such a thing as a finite self at all, but only perhaps a series of states of consciousness. Consciousness itself is in this case apparently identified with the Absolute, so that this series of states is *within* the Absolute Whose experiences it constitutes.

It has been observed[1] that mystics of other lands (for example Henri Frédéric Amiel) have enjoyed similar subjective experiences which they have found satisfying. Amiel, in his *Journal Intime*, speaks of thought being dissolved in 'l'immuable repos du Rien', and of the Absolute as being 'le Zero de toute détermination'. It is worth noting that 'Zero' in Indian mathematics, as Betty Heimann has shown, does not mean what it does in British mathematics, but something more positive. There is ample opportunity for misunderstanding here.

Two questions fall to be answered at this point:

(1) *Why, if the Buddha was a Hindu, did Buddhism become a separate international movement?*

In answer it may be said that viewed from one aspect Buddhism *is* Hinduism, enlarged and divested of its social and institutional frame-

1 Whether Amiel's experience is entirely an independent one is perhaps open to question. A perusal of the *Journal Intimate* shows that its most 'oriental' passages are

work (caste and sacrificial ritual) and so adapted for export purposes. Asia acknowledges in many ways a great debt to India. Indian colonial expansion covers a period of 1,300 years, as long as that which separates modern England from the days of Ethelbert of Kent. During that period the great empire of the Sailendra dynasty covered the whole of Malaysia, and it was Buddhist. In the ninth century A.D., the Cambojan empire also arose and lasted for 400 years, with its capital at Angkor the Magnificent, a city of a million inhabitants, larger and more splendid, it has been said, than Rome in the days of the Cæsars. This too gained its inspiration from India, and although at first the influence was Hindu, it gradually became Buddhist. The early colonies seem to have been Brahmanical and non-Buddhist, but the liberal or Mahayana type of Buddhism came later, and being tolerant and adaptable, it existed side by side with ordinary Hinduism, and some pockets of the latter, such as Bali, have remained entirely Hindu to this day.

Thus outside India it seems that Indian influence ultimately became predominantly Buddhist, and for a very obvious reason. Hinduism, dependent as it is upon the accepted dominance of the Brahmin caste as a hereditary spiritual aristocracy, is tied to the country of its origin. To this day, Brahmins are not at ease in a foreign country. One of them told me recently that although he was allowed to come to Europe, he would have to engage in a long fast and penances on his return to India, in order to expiate his transgression of so many strict Hindu rules during his sojourn abroad. But Gautama cut clean away from this kind of fetter. Though himself a Kshatriya, caste with him did not count, and his teaching about sacrifice, whether we have it verbatim or not, is well reflected in such a passage as the following, from the *Samyutta*, i, 169:

> I lay no wood, brahmin, for fires on altars.
> Only within burneth the fire I kindle.
> Ever my fire burns: ever tense and ardent.
> I, Arahant, work out the life that's holy.
> . . . the heart's the altar,
> The fire thereon, this is man's self, well tamed.

Buddhism, even in its liberal or Mahayana form, has no real sacrifice, only honorific offerings before the statue of the Buddha. It has no

associated with his reading of Schopenhauer—who was, of course, deeply influenced by Indian thought. Amiel self-consciously refers to 'the Buddhist tendency in me' as gathering strength year by year, and this would seem to show that he actually recognised the source from which he derived it.

priesthood, but only monks; and its doctrine of *bodhisattvas*, or beings who are recurrent incarnations of the cosmic Buddha-Spirit, has enabled it to annex the pantheons of China and Japan, and to turn their members into respectable Buddhist saints.

(2) *Why, if the Buddha was a Hindu, has Buddhism almost died out in India?*

Probably there are three main reasons.

First, the animosity of the vested interest of the Brahmin caste. So strong was this body, that although it made valiant efforts to adopt the Buddha into its system, it found his teaching an indigestible morsel. There are said to be still eleven millions of Buddhists somewhere in India,[2] according to a recent census, but this may be due to modern immigrations from farther east, or to modern propaganda.

Second, the tendency of the Buddhists to use the laity less. The Jain laity are an active and comparatively strong element in Indian life; but Buddhism in medieval India shut itself up more and more in the cloister. Thus when we come to:

Three, the Moslem invasions, we find that the destruction of the Buddhist monasteries and the massacre of their inmates left practically no one to carry on the dissemination of Buddhist teaching.

Some writers have compared Gautama in his relation to Hinduism with Luther in relation to the Catholic Church; but the analogy is hardly a good one, since Luther retained a great deal of medieval thought and practice, and Catholicism was not a national religion. Almost a better analogy would be the relation of Christ to Judaism, since here there was a real breach with a nationalist system, and a rejection of ritual practices; and this enabled all that was best in Judaism to become internationalised, and available for all Gentiles. Yet it seems probable that Gautama never thought of himself as the founder of a new system, but only as the reformer of an old one.

* * * * *

In general, what is so remarkable about these movements during the philosophical stage of Hinduism is the keen intellectual interest which they pre-suppose. It seems safe to assume that although large masses of the people remained untouched, there was a substantial section of the population which was able to appreciate the penetrating analysis of life and its elements attributed to the Upanishadic teachers, to the Jains, and to Gautama and his friends. This appreciation remains even

[2] Dr. Heimann gives quite different figures!

to the present day, and visitors to India have often remarked upon the readiness of the average Indian to engage in subtle theological and philosophical disputations. It is probable that although Buddhism as a separate movement now seems negligible in India, it has had its effect on Hinduism, which, with its extraordinarily absorbent and syncretistic capacities, has assimilated the movement begun by Gautama into itself without any major conflict, and without persecution. The slaughter of animals for sacrifice has declined. The ethical side of Gautama's teaching, so much stronger than that of the ordinary Upanishadic sages, has not been without its effects. Brahminism has even allowed Gautama to enter its system as an *avatar* or discontinuous incarnation (*see* Chapter 5); and it seems likely that the accession of Brahmin disciples to what began as a movement among Kshatriyas may have been one of the contributory causes which led to the development of the Mahayana or liberal type of Buddhism outside India. Nehru gives it as his opinion that an increased emphasis in Hinduism upon the world-negating ascetic element in life was actually the result of the Buddhist movement. The idea of the value of other-worldliness had always been present in India, but before the time of the Buddha there had been more of the old Aryan ideal of a full and all-rounded life with the first part of it spent in ordinary mundane activities, and only old age reserved for complete withdrawal from life's normal attachments. Gautama's own early withdrawal set the example of a new kind of proportion, and altered the balance between life-affirmation and life-negation. Vast communities of monks and nuns developed, and it has been pointed out that the very name of Bihar[3] today is derived from the word Vihara, indicating how full of monastic houses that great area must have been.

Another effect of the Buddhist movement in India is said to have been a stiffening of the caste system, and the development of the untouchables. In the days of Gautama it seems likely that the Brahmins were the only rigid caste. The Kshatriyas were tolerant, and ready to incorporate suitable individuals irrespective of their birth. The Vaisyas were the largest class, and were then agriculturists, whereas today they are merchants and tradesmen. But the effect of Jainism and Buddhism was to discredit the life of the agriculturalist, since it involved to a considerable degree the destruction of organic life. Hence

3 *Vihara* is the usual word for a Buddhist community house.
   Compare in England the curious phrase 'sele Suffolk' as applied to the East-Anglian county. 'Sele' is 'selig' or 'holy' and the appellation was bestowed because of the vast numbers of rich churches and religious houses with which it was dotted during the Middle Ages.

agriculture went down in the social scale, and came to be regarded as a menial and disreputable occupation, and those who lived on the land became correspondingly degraded. This was not, of course, at all what the Buddha himself had intended, but he unwittingly helped in the process.

Gautama was not an extremist, but an eminently practical soul. Thus his reaction against the excessive mortifications of the flesh which he found prevailing among the Jains led him to direct his disciples to perform their daily period of meditation, not fasting, but after a light midday meal. He calls his system the Middle Path (i.e., the golden mean, or the rightly proportioned way between self-indulgence and severe asceticism), and thus reminds us of Aristotle and his Ethics. Gautama is a penetrating thinker, but he will never allow himself to be dragged into the discussion of hair-splitting metaphysical subtleties, or trapped into making admissions about things which cannot truly be known. Life is to him the important thing, and *metta*, which means universal benevolence or active goodwill—('togetherness'), is the important virtue.[4]

This emphasis upon a positive ethic sharply separates Buddhism from Hinduism of the standard pattern, and here is the point at which to evaluate the difference. Hinduism sets forth knowledge—seeing the truth—as the way to salvation. But this is not salvation from wickedness or wrongdoing, which is the fruit of self-centredness, but salvation from ignorance. The moment a man knows himself to be one with the Atman-Brahman, he is released. But this has no sort of relation to moral regeneration. To be wise is more important than to be good, since good and evil seem to belong to the sphere of illusion from which wisdom sets one free. It is true that occasionally (*Katha Up.* i, 2.24) one finds suggestions that one cannot attain to knowledge without the preparatory discipline of a well-ordered moral life, but this is not the general teaching of the Upanishads.

The latter is more truly expressed in the following passages:

(1) *Kaushitaki Up.* 3.1. Here we read of the ethnic deity Indra, who has wrought a number of ruthless and devastating actions, presumably in an electric storm, telling a disciple, Pratardana: 'He who understands Me—by no deed of his is the world injured, not by stealing, not by killing an embryo, not by the murder of his mother, not by the murder of his father; if he has done any evil, the dark colour need not depart from his face' (i.e., he need not grow pale with guilt).

(2) *Brihadaranyaka Up.* 4.3.22. 'For the man who desires the Self'—

4 From the same root as English 'amity': cf. German 'mit': Latin 'amicitia'.

says Yajñavalkya, 'then is a father not a father, a mother not a mother, then are the worlds not worlds, the gods not gods, the devas not devas. Then is a thief not a thief, a murderer not a murderer. He is not followed by good or followed by evil, for he has then overcome all the sorrows of the heart.'

Buddhism on the other hand made much of 'right conduct' as a definite element in its Noble Eightfold Path.

The Bhagavadgita, which will be dealt with in the next chapter, made some attempt to bring in an emphasis upon duty or *dharma*, which certainly belonged to earlier Indian religion, and upon which Gautama laid great stress, declaring that the eightfold Aryan path prescribed a moral *dharma* as the prerequisite for the attainment of bliss or Nirvana.

The celebrated Hindu code known as *The Laws of Manu*, though traditionally very ancient, and doubtless containing materials of great antiquity, belongs, in the form in which we know it, to this period, and may date from anywhere between 200 B.C. and A.D. 200. It is the charter of Brahmin domination, and gives an extraordinarily exalted status to that caste; it also proclaims the divine right of kings. But the code is a curious mixture, and while much of it reminds one of the ancient Sumerian legal formulae, it also shows Jain influence in its condemnation of agriculture as injurious to organic life, and stresses the extreme value of asceticism. Taken as a whole it mainifests the effect of Buddhist teaching in its ethicising of the world-renouncing life.

BOOKS FOR FURTHER STUDY

MRS. SINCLAIR STEVENSON. *The Heart of Jainism*. Oxford.

PROFESSOR J. B. PRATT. *India and its Faiths*. Macmillans. 1915.
   The Pilgrimage of Buddhism. Macmillans. 1928.

MRS. RHYS DAVIDS. *A Manual of Buddhism*. Sheldon Press. 1932.

G. C. LOUNSBERY. *Buddhist Meditation in the Southern School*. Kegan Paul. 1935.

PROFESSOR DASGUPTA. Op. cit.

5

THE CHANGE TO INCARNATIONAL RELIGION
THE GREAT EPICS. THE BHAGAVADGITA
THE BEGINNINGS OF BHAKTI

For some reason not fully explained, Indians have not had a strong sense of the value of recording and interpreting the course of events. In the huge mass of Indian literature there is almost nothing corresponding to the works of Thucydides or Tacitus, the Chinese historical records, or even the Anglo-Saxon chronicle.[1] Nor is there biography; nor anything like collections of family or national portraits. This tendency to ignore history has produced, according to Nehru: 'a vagueness of outlook, a divorce from life as it is, a credulity, a "woolliness" of the mind where fact is concerned. That mind was not at all "woolly" in the far more difficult, but inevitably vaguer and more indefinite realms of philosophy; it was both analytic and synthetic, often very critical, sometimes sceptical. But where fact was concerned it was uncritical, because perhaps it did not attach much importance to fact as such.'[2] Those Hindus who concentrate their attention upon the sacred books which have just been described never refer to concrete events in life, but remain wholly absorbed in the invisible and the abstract.

Yet of course historical events did take place, and it is necessary at

[1] Prince Bhanj Deo objects here that there may have been historical records which were destroyed during the sack of Delhi. (*See* p. 98)

[2] Nehru, op. cit. p. 75. So also Dr. Somervell (*After Everest*, p. 306) who has spent many years living in close and friendly contact with Indians: 'Whether events actually occurred or are mere legends and inventions seems to trouble many Indians not at all, and obviously fantastic myths are accepted by the public as possessing equal validity with undoubted historic facts.'

this point to give a brief summary of various important happenings which have helped to mould Hinduism into what, after the days of the Buddha and his immediate followers, it eventually became.

First, in the middle of the fourth century B.C., there were the Greek invasions. As such they were not very substantial affairs, little more perhaps than large border raids, and they were so stoutly resisted by the local kings (for India was then a series of states), that Alexander had to call a halt, and consider whether to go on. In 323 B.C. he died at Babylon, and one of his generals, Seleucus, decided to pursue the campaign, and crossed the Indus with a fresh army. But he was defeated by a powerful king, Chandragupta Maurya, who at the time of Alexander's invasion itself had been in exile. He and his Brahmin minister, Chanakya, went and conferred with Alexander, and were greatly impressed by his plans and personality. When Seleucus entered India, Chandragupta raised a great movement on the basis of patriotism, defeated Seleucus, and forced him to withdraw his Greek garrisons, to make a favourable treaty, and to give him his daughter in marriage.

The chief parts of India ceded to the Indian king were those around what is now Afghanistan and the North-West Frontier, an area which at that time was counted as part of India itself. Chandragupta Maurya established a great empire which covered the whole of the country from the Arabian Sea to the Bay of Bengal, and extended as far north as Kabul. The Maurya dynasty lasted for several generations, and intercourse with Greece continued, an ambassador being sent by Seleucus to the Indian court, whose name was Megasthenes, and who has left us a written account of what he saw there.

The grandson of Chandragupta, Asoka, was a great patron of early Buddhism. Indeed so enthusiastic was he that he erected inscribed pillars in various parts of his dominions advocating its principles. He himself did not become a monk, and it is suggested that this early Buddhism was much more of a lay movement, and far less monastic than it became later on; and that in spite of its doctrines it did not inhibit the world-affirming tendencies of ordinary human nature any more than Christianity. Perhaps Asoka himself may be said to have resembled a tertiary of the Franciscan movement, such as Louis IX of France.[3] He died in 232 B.C., and after his time the Maurya empire gradually faded away, and gave place in the North and Central areas to the Sanga dynasty, which ruled over a smaller territory, in the South

3 Professor Dasgupta is of the opinion that the personal faith of Asoka is the parent of the idea of the oneness of all religion, which we find expressed by cultured Indians, especially at the present day.

to a number of separate states, and in the extreme North to an Indo-Greek Bactrian kingdom, extending from Kabul to the Punjab. A Greek king of this state, Menander by name, appears in Buddhist literature as the 'King Milinda', who asked questions and sought instruction. Greeks, however, did not confine their attentions to Buddhism. One, at least, became a prominent Vaishnavite Hindu, and has left us an inscription written in Sanskrit:

'This Garuda column of Vasudeva, the God of gods, was erected by Heliodorus, a worshipper of Vishnu, the son of Dion, and an inhabitant of Taxila, who came as Greek ambassador from the great King Antalcidas to King Kashiputra Bhagabhadra, the saviour, then reigning in the fourteenth year of his kingship.

'Three immortal precepts, when practised well, lead to heaven—self-restraint, self-sacrifice, and conscientiousness.'

*   *   *   *   *

Meanwhile Scythian invaders from Central Asia established themselves in the Oxus valley, and then a Mongolian people, the Yueh Chih, pushed them out from thence and drove them over into India, where they settled in the North, and became converts to Hinduism, and some of them also to Buddhism. Next, a clan of the Yueh Chih, the Kushans, invaded India, defeated the Scythians and pushed them still farther down into Kathiawar and the Deccan. These Kushans created a large and fairly stable empire over the whole of North India and part of Central Asia. Their principal king was Kanishka, who was converted to Buddhism, and it was at this period that the great schism occurred, which permanently divided the Buddhists into two separate groups. But the Kushan empire eventually had to give way in the face of a new nationalist leader, also called Chandragupta, who about A.D. 320 drove out new waves of these invaders and set up what is known as the Gupta empire. This lasted for about 300 years, and during half that time was most properous and powerful. Its sway was in the end interrupted by an invasion of Hunnish Mongols, which however was of brief duration. Thereafter the story of Hinduism becomes crossed by the gradual influx of Moslem power and influence, which must be our concern in a later chapter.

For the present we must concentrate our attention upon the religious developments which belong to the somewhat chequered period that has just been described. Apart from the growth and expansion of the Buddhist movement, the most striking feature is what may be described as *the theistic reaction*.

Upanishadic doctrine, as we have seen, tended more and more to depersonalise the idea of Deity, and its logical outcome may be seen in the religious philosophy of the Buddhist and Jain movements. Whether the oscillation away from this would have come in any case, or whether it was encouraged by the new and cruder methods of population which now come flooding in, we cannot tell. What is certain, however, is that from about 250 B.C. onwards, traces of a different attitude towards Deity and different conceptions of the Godhead become apparent, as, for example, in the later Upanishads. Instead of non-duality, we get Deity set over against the soul and the world, and instead of the impersonal title of Brahman, we get the use of a more personal word, Iswara, or Lord. This movement seems chiefly to centre round a particular Vedic solar deity, Vishnu, who, although known long before, now assumes greater prominence. The origin of this Vaishnavite religion, which is almost like something new coming into Hinduism, is still obscure. Some have seen in it the work of a special prophet or teacher, Vasudeva, but we can discover next to nothing about him, and as we have already seen, in the inscription of Heliodorus the word Vasudeva is an epithet of Vishnu himself.

It is not quite accurate to say that this Indian theism is always associated with the idea of incarnation. Theism need not necessarily be so, as we see in the case of Islam, and it is more correct to say that though the idea of incarnation requires theism as a basis, and though the idea gradually developed in Vaishnavism, it was not there from the first, and from other forms of Indian theism it is markedly absent.

We have now to consider some of the chief literature in which this theistic doctrine finds expression. It comprises first, the two great epics, the Ramayana and the Mahabharata. Let us, however, not be misunderstood: the epics themselves are the growth of centuries, and are themselves much older than the doctrine. Although it is impossible to date them with any accuracy, they certainly go back to the pre-Buddhist period. It is the later use which is made of them that concerns us here.

The *Ramayana* is the story of the career of an ideal king, Rama, and his consort Sita, who is the pattern of wifely fidelity and sweetness. It is of enormous length, and contains 500 cantos and 24,000 couplets; and it has been rendered, with variations and additions, into the chief languages of India, and is still read by thousands of Hindus, not merely as fine literature, but as possessing a certain sacred quality. The original Ramayana was the work of the poet Valmiki, and was written in Sanskrit, but the rendering which has the greatest distinction and also the most religious significance is the work of Tulsi Das, the sixteenth-century poet (*see* Chapter 7). In the earlier recensions Rama appears as wholly human, but as time passes he is accepted as the descent of a Divine Being to earth in human guise. This descent is called in Sanskrit *avatar*, and the appearance of the concept of an *avatar* marks an important development in Indian religion. It is doubtful at what date the word first occurs with this precise meaning, but negatively it is significant that from a Sanskrit glossary of the older Upanishads it is completely absent. The idea is, however, clearly present in the popular religion of about the second century B.C., and it is significant that it appears, just about the same time, as a vital element in liberal or Mahayana Buddhism. The conjecture has been made that the idea of a discontinuous descent of a Divine Being in human form to help and save mankind originated somewhere outside India, perhaps in the north-east of Iran, and that it became diffused eastward and westward from this area. Certainly there is a scripture called the Bahram Yasht which has a list of incarnate appearances of an Iranian divinity called Verethragna, most of which are sub-human, though one is human. Verethragna can hardly be the same as Vishnu, though in India Vishnu has a number of *avatars* (some say twenty-four), of which the first five are sub-human, but the sixth is a human figure, Rama with the axe. Yet Verethragna is apparently the same as Vrttrahan, 'the victorious one', which is an epithet applied to another Vedic god, Indra, and since the Vedic gods gradually become fused and interchangeable, and may in any case be addressed with similar adjectives, it seems quite likely that we have here in Iran an earlier example of the *avatar* idea. Again, Mahayana or liberal Buddhism develops the idea of a succession of incarnations or *bodhisattvas* of the Cosmic Buddha-Spirit, for the help of suffering mankind. Of these an important one is Amitabha, and Sir Charles Eliot gives reasons for thinking that at least this particular *bodhisattva*, if not some others, has strong affinities with a being found in Zoroastrian beliefs.

At any rate, wherever it originated, this idea of a discontinuous incarnation is certainly as much present in India as it was in the Hellenistic world of St. Paul's day. The main differences are that in India the *avatar* is surrounded by myth and legend, whereas in Christendom, apart from the apocryphal gospels, the incarnation of Christ is strictly historical; and again[4] that in India the appearances of the Godhead in

4 Eliot points out that about the time of the rise of Christianity, South India appears to have been a civilised country which, from the various references in classical literature, seems to have maintained commercial relations with Rome. Op. cit. p. 214.

the flesh are not invariably human, and are certainly plural in number, while they present the form of a visionary illusion, a mere appearance rather than a fleshly reality, and this, which Christians called a docetic incarnation (Greek δοκέω, I seem), was at an early date condemned by the authorities of the Church as being heretical and false teaching.[5] In Christianity the incarnation is not multiple, but 'once-for-all', and is never sub-human, the Self-Expression or Logos of God reaching its peak in the life of Jesus of Nazareth, in whom alone 'dwelt all the fullness of the Godhead bodily'.

The second great epic, the *Mahabharata*, is even longer than the Ramayana, and contains 90,000 couplets, so that it is about seven times the size of the Iliad and Odyssey put together. The theme in this case is a great war between two opposing alliances of North-Indian tribes. The heroes, like those of Homer, are all god-born chiefs, and the rivalry between two of them, Arjuna and Karna, which is a leading *motif* in the epic, recalls the rivalry between Achilles and Hector in the pages of the *Iliad*. What for our purpose is important is that within the boundaries of this vast poem are to be found two cantos (as well as other passages) which have a definite religious message, the Bhagavadgita, or Song of the Lord (*Mahab. VI*), and the Narayaniya (*Mahab. XI*). Both these sections, and others as well, are in form like metrical Upanishads. The Gita is the more celebrated, and though it forms a definite part of the epic, it is frequently treated as an independent work, and is published separately in numerous editions with and without commentary.

*   *   *   *   *

The Bhagavadgita. The poem is relatively short—some 700 verses, but it is the most important single document in the whole of Hinduism. Innumerable treatises have been written upon it, and fresh editions are continually appearing. So highly esteemed is it that it is used, like the New Testament and the Qur'an, for the administration of oaths in law-courts. Opinions differ as to its date and composition. Since Kalidasa, who lived about A.D. 400, quotes from it, it can be as late as that date, but the most recent scholarship inclines to the view that it was composed in its original form a little earlier than the Christian era, and that in its final form it cannot be later than the second century A.D. It is now considered improbable (if not quite impossible) that it con-

---

5 *See the Epistle of Ignatius, Bishop of Antioch, to the Trallians*, in which he says: 'stop your ears when anyone speaks to you apart from Jesus Christ. . . . Who was *truly* born and ate and drank, etc., etc.'

tains any traces of borrowing from Christianity. As to its unity, there is sharp division of opinion. Garbe, and more recently Rudolf Otto, have held the view that it is possible to detect definite strata in the *textus receptus*, and Otto, in particular, has split it up into eight divisions:

> The original Gita;
> Sāmkhya additions;
> Brahman glosses;
> Bhakti glosses;
> A Yoga treatise;
> A mythological gloss;
> An Advaita gloss;
> A hymn in praise of Krishna.

Such a stratification may seem to involve overmuch subjective prejudice, and E. J. Thomas considers it quite possible, making allowance for the Hindu temperament, that the various doctrines which the Gita contains may have all been taught by one man. But when we consider the probable manner in which the Upanishads grew up as separate wholes, it becomes reasonable to think that a similar accumulation of heterogeneous matters may have resulted in the shape of the Gita as we see it today. Garbe's view is that the original Gita belongs to about 200 B.C., and that, like parts of the late Svetasvatara Upanishad, it is theistic in its outlook. He holds that in the second century A.D. it underwent a revision in the interests of schools of monistic philosophy and that these interpolations amount to about one-fifth of the whole poem. The alternative view is that the monistic portions represent parts of an old verse Upanishad of a date rather later than that of the Svetasvatara, which has been worked over in the interests of theism into the present Gita, so as to enable devotees of Vishnu to express their feelings in philosophic terms. The doctrine of the poem thus admits of being described (in the words of E. J. Thomas) as 'a mitigated pantheism'. At any rate, as material for meditation it soon won its way, and no one who wishes to understand the religion of the enlightened Hindu can afford to neglect reading it. Gandhi himself declared that he found immense refreshment of spirit and lofty inspiration from a frequent resort to its pages. It has all the advantages of a brief manual of theology, since it contains the quintessence of the Upanishadic philosophical theories, and is, therefore, a convenient substitute for meandering through these often obscure and very miscellaneous works. But it contains certain items which the Upanishads in general do not possess:

(1) The conception of a Personal Lord and Master to Whom loving devotion is due;

(2) The conception of discontinuous incarnation;

(3) The doctrine that ordinary daily life in the world, as lived there with a certain detachment of spirit, can be a good and adequate life, and that there is no need to go into the cloister or jungle in order to be virtuous and pious.

These three ideas form an immensely important contribution to the religious life of India, and as far as they go, they provide a gracious and spiritual way for her people. There was a period when the Gita was largely forgotten, but for many years now it has recovered its favour, and nationalist enthusiasm has tended to enthrone it in the hearts of Hindus as a worthy rival of the New Testament.

Such a valuation makes a closer scrutiny of the Bhagavadgita imperative. The story it tells is a simple one. Arjuna, one of the sons of King Pandu, is about to give battle, when, like Hamlet, he is halted by his divided thoughts, for the folk he is about to slay are his own kinsmen. His bow slips from his hand, he stays his chariot, and sinks back into his seat dejected, between the two armies. His charioteer, Hrishikesa, then addresses him, and in a long dialogue gives him words of advice. But Hrishikesa is really the Bhagava, Krishna Vasudeva, who is an *avatar* of Vishnu the kindly God, and soon the human incarnation is forgotten, and it is the Divine Lord Who speaks. The central doctrine which he imparts is that one can find true happiness in the performance of action without attachment. 'He who places his actions on Brahma, who abandons attachment, and thus acts, is not stained by sin, and is like a lotus leaf unstained by water.' One should pursue the duties of one's station in life with complete indifference as to the result. It is Arjuna's duty as a Kshatriya to do his part as a warrior and this he must do, regardless of the consequences. In any case, since the slayer and the slain are both Brahma, and Brahma slays not nor is slain (for Brahma is self-existent and imperishable), there is nothing to make one shrink from taking part in a battle.

Side by side with this, as it seems, rather cold-blooded doctrine is put an earnest appeal to the disciple to serve God as a Personal Saviour and Friend: 'Have thy mind on Me, be devoted to Me. To Me thou shalt come; what is true I promise; dear art thou to Me,' and again: 'They who worship this righteous immortal teaching as I have uttered it, full of faith, making Me their supreme object, they to Me are surpassingly dear.'

The two principles seem quite inconsistent, but that is perhaps the reason for the wide appeal of the Gita. It brings together two seemingly incompatible elements, emotional devotion and philosophic detachment, and declares that both are legitimate elements in the religious life. Moreover the Indian mind has (as has been said) a complete disregard for 'the law of the excluded middle'.

But this is not all. Set in the very centre of the Gita is a treatise on the technique of meditation which has become the charter of Hindu contemplatives, and of which a section may here be quoted.

Bhag. VI, 10 ff.: 'A Yogi should constantly train his self, staying in a secret place, alone, controlling his mind, free from hope and possessions. In a pure place, setting up for himself a firm seat, not too high, not too low, with cloth, antelope skin, and kusa grass upon it, there bringing his mind to one point, restraining the action of the mind and the senses, and sitting on the seat, he should practise Yoga for the purifying of the self. Holding his body, head, and neck evenly, firm without motion, looking at the point of his nose, and not looking round about him.

'With his self at peace, freed from fear, abiding in the vow of celibacy, restraining his mind, trained with his thought on Me, let him sit intent on Me. Thus ever training his self, the Yogi with mind restrained attains to peace, to the highest nirvana, which exists in Me.

'Yoga is not for one who eats too much, nor for one who fasts excessively, nor for one of very sleepy habit, nor for the sleepless, O Arjuna.

'For him who is trained in food and recreation, whose activities are trained in performing actions, who is trained in sleeping and in waking, Yoga becomes a destroyer of pain.

'When his mind is restrained and fixed on the Self, without longing for any desires, then he is called trained.

'As a lamp in a windless place flickers not, so is this deemed to be a likeness of the Yogi of restrained mind, who practises Yoga of the Self.'

And finally, there is the famous declaration of Vishnu, wearing the form of Krishna: 'Though I am the Unborn, the changing Self, though Lord of creatures, I condition my own nature, and am born by My supernatural power. Whenever there is a decay of righteousness . . . and a rising of unrighteousness, then I emit Myself. In order to save the good, and to destroy evil-doers; to establish righteousness I am born from age to age. He who knows this, when he comes to die is not reborn, but comes to Me.'

In the eleventh section of the Gita is a superb rhapsodical passage, in which Arjuna declares his vision of God, using all the characteristic language of mystical ecstasy. But the curious feature of this vision

F

which he sees is that it is not entirely the spectacle of a benevolent and gentle deity, but of One Who is both ruthless and terrifying:

> 'Thy mighty form with many mouths beholding,
> O mighty-armed, with eyes, arms, thighs, and feet,
> With many bellies, and many dreadful fangs,
> The worlds all tremble, even as I do also.
>
> As moths in rapid flight too swiftly rushing
> A blazing flame to their destruction enter,
> So do the worlds in flight too swiftly rushing
> Into thy mouths to their destruction enter.
> Thou lickest up and swallowest entirely
> The worlds around, with blazing mouths devouring;
> The entire universe with light thou fillest;
> The dreadful rays of thine blaze forth, O Vishnu.
> Tell me, O thou of dreadful form, who art thou?'[6]

Usually this kind of vision is associated in Hinduism with another cult, to which we must attend presently that of Siva, the terrible personification of Life in its harshest mood. How is this? The answer is that Hinduism always keeps its eyes fixed on Organic Nature 'red in tooth and claw with ravine'. It deifies and venerates the destructive and generative forces of the world, and readily accepts the idea of a Supreme Being Who is beyond all moral values. Hence, any affirmations of a high moral tone which it may seem to make from time to time rather tend to lose their force. This is its dilemma. It can never quite make up its mind to choose the ethical in preference to the ethnic, and so it remains to the end, as has been said, 'a religion without a wholly integrated personality'. The Buddha seems to have rejected this feature of Hinduism, and to have insisted upon the loftiest ethical principles as being more essential to the good life than an exact doctrine of God. In this respect he stands on the same side as Christians.

*   *   *   *   *

The principle of loving devotion to a personal God is called in India *bhakti*, and from the time when the Gita began to be known, right up to the present day, it has been a most popular element in the devotional life of Hindus. To many of them, no doubt, it has seemed a welcome relief from the rather rarefied intellectual atmosphere of philosophical theology. The scale on which it has expressed itself is

6 These translations are from the English rendering, 'The Song of the Lord', by E. J. Thomas. There are many other versions.

gigantic, and we shall note, as we progress, the vast multitude of quasi-evangelical hymns which have at various times been composed by its votaries. To medieval Hinduism then, let us next pass.

Additional Note on the Gita:

Prince Deo has drawn my attention to the following alternat tv theory as to its origin and growth in authority. He believes thatfea owes its prestige to the fact that Sankara was believed to have written it commentary on it. But, says Deo, there were several Sankaraçaryas, for the name became an official title after the lifetime of the original Sankara, and was applied to the head or abbot of a monastery or *math* which the original Sankara had founded. It was one of these later teachers who wrote the commentary, and thus gave the Gita a much greater authority than it really possessed. Deo thinks that as a composition it is relatively late, not much earlier than the time of Kalidasa, and that it was composed in order to furnish a primitive sanction for its central doctrine, the legitimacy of killing in battle. It is, we might almost say, a pious forgery, a hotch-potch of various mutually incompatible doctrines, and the Brahmins were quite within their rights in refusing to treat it as *śruti* or canonical. On this showing, Deo holds that the present popularity of the Gita may in time decline, and give way before a return to the Upanishads (cf. with this the curious temporary popularity of the Mystical Theology of pseudo-Dionysius the Areopagite in medieval Europe, which was largely due to the erroneous belief that it was the work of an early disciple of St. Paul).

BOOKS FOR FURTHER STUDY

PROFESSOR SARVEPALLI RADHAKRISHNAN. *Indian Philosophy*. Allen and Unwin. London. 1923.

PROFESSOR FRANKLIN EDGERTON. *The Bhagavadgita, text, translations, and commentary*. Two vols. Harvard Oriental Series. 1944.

E. J. THOMAS. *The Song of the Lord*. John Murray. 1931.

SRI AUROBINDO GHOSE. *The Gita*. London. 1938.

ROMESH DUTT. *The Ramayana and the Mahabharata*. Everyman Library. Dent. 1929.

NICOL MACNICOL. *Hindu Scriptures*. Everyman Library. Dent. 1938.

RUDOLF OTTO. *The Original Gita*. London. 1939.

6

HINDUISM DURING THE MEDIEVAL PERIOD

SANKARA, RAMANUJA, AND

THE GROWTH OF BHAKTI

We may begin this chapter by setting down a number of miscellaneous points which have not hitherto been recorded.

(1) It is often maintained that iconographic worship came to India through contact with Greece. Vedic religion was devoid of all forms of idol-and-image-worship, and its cultus usually took place in the open, or in dwelling-houses, not in temples. Early Buddhism was free from idolatry, and there was even a prohibition against making likenesses of the Buddha. Yet Graeco-Bactrian influence seems to have made its way in, and the earliest Buddhist statuary shows traces of it. Curiously enough the word for an image in Persian and Hindustani is *but*, derived from the word Buddha, and the term of contempt used by Moslems for Hindus is *but-parast*, 'image-worshipper'. It is probable that the Dravidians had image-worship, as figurines have been found in the Indus valley excavations which seem to have possessed a religious significance; this would mean that iconolatry, though not practised by the proto-Nordic invaders, was introduced into India by the Dravidian immigrants, who shared it with the entire culture-province of the Middle East and Eastern Mediterranean.

(2) Some time after the composition of the Gita there came into existence a division or classification of Hindu sacred literature into *śruti*, 'that which has been heard' (i.e., revealed), and *smriti*, 'that which has been handed down' (i.e., human tradition). This division evidently arose out of the theistic movement, since the *smriti*, which includes the epics and the *puranas* or sectarian books, may be called in general

theistic literature, while the *śruti* or canonical books are the Vedas and Upanishads. Strict Brahmins do not regard anything in the second group as *śruti*, no matter how sacred or edifying, and this shows clearly that the true Brahmanical doctrine is of the nature of a monistic Pantheism. (But today the Gita is often treated as *śruti*.)

(3) This has not hindered vast numbers of Hindus from becoming either 'mitigated pantheists' or definite theists, and the Brahmins have evidently tolerated this situation so long as their own prestige and authority continue to be recognised.

(4) Between the defeat of the Greeks and the Moslem invasions, i.e., from about 300 B.C. to A.D. 1000, a large part of India enjoyed orderly and settled government extending over several centuries. It was during this time that colonisation went on, and it is also clear that the heads of the various states had Brahmin ministers and advisers, and that these Brahmins saw to it that in the different realms over which their masters ruled, Hinduism was, so to speak, the established religion; but in order to effect this, they made considerable concessions to the popular cults, and so long as the caste system was respected, and the proper place was given to their own order and its claims, they were ready to tolerate a good deal of what may be called mass-superstition, and the continuance of practices which had no connexion at all with the loftier Upanishadic teaching. A rough analogy to this may be seen in medieval Europe, where Latin Christianity was fairly tolerant towards local customs, so long as the Papal claims were acknowledged, and the Christian hierarchy and the monastic orders respected.[1]

The net result of all this has been that Hinduism has gradually become what it is today, an enormously tolerant and inclusive institution. Yet the dominant features of it since (say) the year A.D. 600 have been (1) sectarian theistic devotion or *bhakti* of an emotional character, (2) the persistence and elaboration of that world-renouncing asceticism to which Buddhism seems to have given such an increased impetus. Sri Aurobindo, the well-known modern Hindu philosopher, actually calls the Buddhist movement a great rebellion of the spiritual against the material.

Sectarian theistic devotion followed two main lines:

[1] The relation of the more philosophical kind of religion to popular superstition is a very controversial one. There can be no doubt that early medieval Christianity made, at least unofficially, very considerable concessions to popular superstition (as, for instance, in Scandinavia and Central Europe) and even the best thirteenth-century bishops, such as Grossetête, had a hard struggle to check ebullitions of latent heathenism in their dioceses. But the spread of literacy in Europe, especially in Protestant countries, has on the whole tended to purify Christianity.

Vaishnavism, or the worship of a single deity as Vishnu, revealed through his *avatars*.

Saivism, or the worship of a single deity as Siva, who has no *avatars*, but only prophets or teachers, and who is the personification of the Life-Force in its most ruthless aspects.[2]

We must consider each of these in turn.

Vaishnavism. Something has already been said about this in the last chapter. Although a hymn to Vishnu is to be found in the first book of the Rig-Veda, it is by no means certain that he is a genuine Vedic god. Przyluski has declared that his name is Dravidian, and he seems to have some associations with beliefs which must be regarded as represented chiefly by those surviving among primitive tribes. Professor Hutton in fact regards him as the fruit of the reaction of what he calls proto-Hinduism to the religion of the Nordic invaders, so that he may represent an adoption into Aryan religion of a deity really belonging to the conquered peoples.[3] Anyhow, Vishnu, Siva and Kali, as we have them, are not Rig-Vedic deities at all, and Vishnu now belongs uncompromisingly to the circle of ideas connected with multiple incarnation. The two favourite *avatars* of Vishnu are Rama and Krishna, but the latter is sometimes identified with other alleged local appearances, as for instance Vitthata or Vithoba, who is really a local divinity of Pandharpur in the Deccan, but has been assimilated to Krishna, without, however, changing his name. The great temple of Jagannath at Puri in Orissa was built in 1198 on the site of a much older cultus to commemorate another manifestation of Vishnu. But Krishnaism is the most popular form of Vaishnavite worship. It appears to have shown considerable syncretistic features from the start, and to have arisen from the fusion of two very diverse traditions, the one represented in the Gita, the other in the salacious stories of the Puranas (q.v.). According to those who hold this view, the historical Krishna was a prophetic teacher rather of the same sort as the Iranian Zarathustra, who proclaimed the worship of one God, called the Bhagavat or the Lord. To this historical character came eventually to be added (i) the idea that he was not merely a teacher

2 This double theism, as Eliot calls it, seems to be peculiar to India, and it is difficult for Europeans to understand. But it seems to present no obstacles to the Indian mind. It is almost, though not quite, the same as the distinction which obtains in Christian countries between those modern Roman Catholics who insist on addressing their main devotions to Mary the Immaculate, and their evangelical Protestant neighbours who are virtually Jesus-worshippers (to the ignoring of God the Father). But since Mary is not a divine being, the analogy must not be pressed.

3 *See* Hutton, appendix on Hinduism and primitive religions in *Caste in India*, p. 201.

but an *avatar*; (ii) the attachment to this *avatar* of the mythology surrounding a rustic fertility god, perhaps the local divinity of an invading tribe of mountain nomads, and bearing the general characteristics of the Greek Pan. Certainly Clement of Alexandria credits the Indians with the worship of Pan, though no evidence has come to light establishing this. On the other hand, the city of Muttra, later a centre of Krishna-worship, was, for a time, under the rule of the Greek king Menander, and was thus brought into touch with the worship of Dionysus, as discoveries of Indo-Greek statuary in that city have revealed. The tales of the Maenads and of the infant Dionysus certainly resemble vaguely the tales of the infant Krishna and of the *gopis* or adoring milkmaids. But we can say no more than this. At any rate Krishna-worship has always been surrounded by a strong erotic, not to say antinomian and sensual, element. Perhaps the efforts of the Brahmins to bring local cults within the pale of an orthodox institution resulted in the amalgamation of four separate deities into one, Vishnu adopting into himself Vasudeva, Krishna, and Narayana; and as we have seen in the case of Vithoba and Jagannath, this process has been further extended. There is evidence that (whether seriously or in mere adulation) King George V and Mahatma Gandhi have both in their day been addressed as Raghubasmani, an epithet which properly belongs to *avatars* of Vishnu.

Alberuni, writing about North-West India in A.D. 1030, has much to say about Vaishnavism, which was at that time even perhaps stronger than its rival, Saivism. This medieval religion rejected the idea of blood-sacrifices, and made the basis of salvation an emotional one, most worship taking the form of hymns, and the offering of flowers. The chief leaders in fostering such a type of liturgy are known as the twelve Aḷwars (pron. Arhwars), but the three earliest of these would seem to be legendary beings. The fourth, Naum'arwar, may have lived in the seventh or eighth century A.D., and we know that by A.D. 100 the hymns of the Aḷwars were being arranged and treated as devotional classics (the Prabandhar or Nalayiram). The whole collection contains 4,000 verses arranged in four parts, and a selection of 602 verses has been edited for daily worship. These assume the veneration of a statue or image, and the liturgy includes the rousing of the god in the morning, with attendance on him during the day, and a general treatment of the image similar to that known to have been practised in Egyptian temples in antiquity.[4]

Saivism: It is fairly easy for Western Christians to understand the

4 A. W. Shorter. *The Egyptian Gods*, p. 25.

worship of Vishnu, since it has, as we can see, several points of contact with the worship of the Incarnate Logos, and in any case Vishnu is usually a benevolent deity. Siva, on the other hand, seems to most observers a really terrifying and dangerous god. According to mythology his eternal home is in the Himalayas, and the great rivers, especially the Ganges, flow from it. A deity exhibiting his attributes was apparently venerated as far back as the hey-day of the proto-Dravidian civilisation in the Indus valley. His earlier name in the Vedas seems to have been Rudra, which may mean 'red' or 'roarer', and sounds like an epithet of the sullen-coloured thundercloud. But although Rudra is mentioned in the Vedas, he is not strictly an Aryan deity, but belongs rather to the people conquered by the Nordics. As time goes on, though he keeps all his attributes, he becomes known by the name of Siva, which means propitious. We naturally recall the renaming of the Erinyes or Greek Furies as the Eumenides ('the kindly and propitious ones'), and the motive behind the renaming is the same doubtless in each case. Siva is plainly the Life-Force personified. In some of his images he is depicted as Natarajan dancing the celestial dance, which typifies the burning zest of life. He becomes associated with the uncanny elements in experience, with what Otto has called 'daemonic dread', and he is reverenced as 'the One who is in the fall of the leaf, the threatener, the slayer, the afflicter'.

All this is realistic enough: and it is easy to understand that the harsher elements in nature which we cannot control should be accepted as due to the inscrutable majesty of a Supreme Being. 'What? Shall we not receive good at the hand of Elohim, and shall we not receive evil?' says Job.

> 'God the All-Terrible, King Who ordainest
> Lightnings Thy messengers, thunder Thy sword.'

is to be found in a Christian hymn-book; but it might just as easily be the beginning of a Saivite hymn. As Eliot says: 'The Creator is also the Destroyer, not in anger, but by the very nature of his activity.' Curiously enough, Siva also represents austerity, because India believes that asceticism means power, and Siva is the personification of power of any and every kind. He is provided with a consort, Kali or Mahadevi, who is even more terrible than her husband, and demands bloody sacrifice. Finally, Siva and his female counterpart, Sakti, stand for sexual energy, for virility and fecundity, and are therefore worshipped under symbols which stand for these things, even though their original significance may have now been forgotten. Indeed, sometimes in the past they have certainly been worshipped with rites which involved licence. (It is, however, quite unfair to say that licentiousness is an integral part of all Hinduism, or that the symbols which had a sexual origin mean anything obscene today to millions of Hindus.)[5]

It is an extraordinary fact that Siva, the violent and dangerous deity, in the medieval period in India becomes refined and sublimated as an object of *bhakti*, more especially in the South. The theory is that the South was never colonised by the Nordics to the same extent as the North, and that the worship of Siva, who, as we have seen, is Dravidian in origin, attained to a fuller development in lands which have remained mainly Dravidian in stock. Be this as it may, it is certainly the case that soon after the first century A.D. we find a number of Saivite religious poems being produced, mainly, though not entirely, as hymns for use in temple worship. A Saivite collection of hymns, the Tirumurai, was made about A.D. 1000, and its contents comprise material which is some centuries earlier, notably the Tiruvaçagam of Manikka-Vaçagar, which Eliot describes as 'the finest devotional poem that India can show,' and which is offered to the god as an act of worship. Manikka-Vaçagar flourished in the eighth century A.D. and was one of a number of Saivite saints, of whom there are said to have been sixty-three. Siva is here addressed as the loving Father (or Mother), Who yearns after human souls.

'With mother-love He came and made me His.'

'O Thou Who art to Thy true servants true.'

'To Thee O Father may I attain, may I yet dwell with Thee.'

These are individual lines which occur in the Tirumurai, and with them we may set some stanzas from a longer poem, which is known as 'The Wonder of Salvation'.[6]

'To me, who toiled and moiled mid fools that knew not way of final peace
He taught the way of pious love; and that bold deeds might cease and flee,
Purging the foulness of my will, made me pure bliss, took for his own;
Twas thus the Father gave me grace; O rapture, who so blest as I?

5 Przyluski holds that both *lingam* (the name for the phallic symbol of Siva) and *puja* (the word for objective worship of a sacrificial character) are words of non-Aryan origin, and therefore probably taken over from the language of pre-Vedic religion.
6 The translation is by Dr. Pope.

'Me trusting every lie as truth, plunged in desire of woman's charms,
He guarded that I perished not with soul perturbed, the Lord Superne,
On Whose left side His consort dwells—He brought me nigh His jewelled
    feet,
Twas thus my Guru gave me grace; O rapture, who so blest as I?

'With those that knew not right or good, men ignorant, I wandered too.
The first, the primal Lord Himself, threefold pollution caused to cease;
Even me He took as something worth—like dog in sumptuous litter borne.
Twas thus the Mother gave me grace; O rapture, who so blest as I?'

Eliot calls these lyrics 'a tropical version of Hymns Ancient and
Modern', but he goes on to point out that the resemblances are really
superficial. They may indicate the hunger of the Indian soul for a
Personal Saviour, but the object of devotion is mythical, not historical,
and the relation between Siva and the soul is not quite dignified
enough, for the attitude of the god to the creaturely is one of *lila*,
sport, or surplus energy, and the grace of Siva does not actually
redeem from moral turpitude, since Siva is not a morally holy god,
but merely delivers from ignorance as to the identity of the soul with
Deity. Moreover, there is no 'passion of Siva', by which he saves the
world. At the same time the possibility of covert Christian influence
cannot be entirely excluded. We know that during the seventh century
Nestorian missionaries introduced Christianity into South India, and
the mere fact of the continued existence to this day in the region of
Travancore of a native Christian church descended from this mission
is proof that it established itself there firmly. Mr. Isaac Tambyah has
maintained with much learning[7] that the development of Saivite hymns
shows the influence of this community, and it is impossible to dismiss
his arguments as trivial. At the same time, the variations in the date
assigned to Manikka-Vaçagar render it difficult to know how much
emphasis to lay upon this. Recent Hindu scholars have placed him in
the second or third century A.D., while Eliot thinks that his poem
reads like an eleventh-century production, and against this it is urged
that a commentary upon the Tiruvaçagam was written about A.D. 700.
    In the thirteenth and fourteenth centuries this devotion to Siva
received a doctrinal basis in what is called the Saiva Siddhanta, by
four Açaryas or doctors of the church. The works of the poet-saints
were in fact followed by those of a number of theologians, who

7 In his 'Hymns of Saivite Saints'. Bishop Neill however doubts the possibility of
influence on the part of the Syrian Christians of Travancore, who, he thinks, lived very
much apart from the general community, 'in a capsule', as he has put it.

proceeded to furnish a doctrinal and philosophical foundation for all this devotion. The outstanding figures are *Sankara* and *Ramanuja*. Sankara lived from 788 to 828, *Ramanuja* about the year 1100. Both are persons of extraordinary interest, but of almost entirely opposite outlook. *Sankara* was a Nambutiri Brahmin of Cochin in Travancore, and his short life of thirty-two years was packed with achievement.[8] A kind of Hindu John Wesley, he travelled over the whole of India, 'arguing, debating, reasoning, convincing, and filling everyone with a part of his own passion and tremendous vitality'. He wrote not only commentaries on the Hindu sacred books, but also popular hymns. He was a curious mixture, part scholar and philosopher, part agnostic, part mystic, part poet and saint, yet withal a competent organiser and a practical reformer. He founded ten religious orders in imitation of the Buddhists—the first to be founded within Brahminism; and, of these, four are still flourishing. He also established four great *maths* or monasteries at the four corners of India. Undoubtedly he had a vision of a united India, but it was of an India not simply at one politically, but also united by sharing a common spiritual culture; and his standard was a very high one. Rudolf Otto has compared and contrasted him with Meister Eckhart. Sankara's teaching is the purest Vedānta philosophy or *Kevala advaita*. According to this, there is only one single Absolute Reality, the Brahman, and outside the Brahman there is nothing which actually and genuinely exists. The entire world which we behold is a cosmic illusion and is misperceived by us—we even misperceive our status in it. It is not until we attain to true knowledge that we find salvation and deliverance from the deception in which we are entangled.

Otto quotes a story from the Vishnu Purana (q.v.) which illustrates this—though it is not told with reference to Sankara. A teacher, Ribhu, came to one Nidagha to instruct him. As Ribhu entered the city, he saw the king, riding on an elephant, accompanied by his attendants. Ribhu asked Nidagha, 'Which is the king?' Nidagha pointed him out, riding on the elephant's back. 'But,' said Ribhu, 'which is the elephant and which is the king?' Nidagha said: 'The king is above and the elephant is below.' 'But,' said Ribhu: 'What is "above", and what is "below"?' Nidagha replied: 'It is as with you and me. You are my teacher and above me. I am your disciple, and below you.' 'But,' said Ribhu: 'Tell me this still: Which of us is I and

8 Sankara himself seems to have been a Saivite, though he was prepared to accept Vaishnavism also. When his mother was dying he recited for her first a hymn to Siva and then one to Vishnu. His followers at the present day have a Saivite bias.

which is you?' Then Nidagha fell down at Ribhu's feet, and exclaimed: 'Truly thou art my master, for no other spirit is so endowed with non-duality as thou. By this I know that thou, my Guru (master), art come.' The comment follows that Nidagha henceforth saw all beings as not distinct from himself.[9]

Some of Sankara's critics declared that he was a Buddhist in disguise. It is certain that the Buddhist movement influenced him much. But, conversely, it is also said that Sankara helped to put an end to Buddhism as a separate movement in India, and this may well have been the case. All the essentials in Buddhism he may have managed to secure within the Brahmin fold. But the story of Ribhu and Nidagha has a strongly Buddhist flavour about it, and greatly resembles the stories connected with the Koans or paradoxes of Dhyana or Zen Buddhism, which was brought into China from India by Bodhidharma about A.D. 527.

Sankara's Advaita Vedanta is still the dominant philosophic outlook native to Hinduism today, and no one can follow Sri Aurobindo's great three-volume exposition, *The Divine Life*, without recognising that it is a valiant attempt to relate the Advaita Vedanta to the modern world of science. It is advisable, however, always to bear in mind that Sankara, like Eckhart, is not to be understood on the basis of mathematics, but of religion. If we stress in religion the priority of God, we approach inevitably to Advaita. If we stress the delegated spontaneity of the creaturely, we separate God from His creation, and move towards theism.

This latter was in effect what *Ramanuja* did (1055-1137). He made no claim to be the founder of a new system, any more than Sankara, although he had a predecessor and master called Yamuna-muni, and his relation to Yamuna has been compared to that existing between Aquinas and Albertus Magnus. Born at Sriperumbudur near Madras, he studied Saivism as a youth, but left it for Vaishnavism. Like his predecessor Sankara, some 300 years earlier, he was a founder of religious orders and is said to have left behind him 700 monasteries. He allowed members of his orders to marry, so that eighty-nine of the abbotships became hereditary. He also visited North India, and according to tradition stayed in Kashmir. Then he retired to Mysore to escape the hostility of a Saivite king, and finally returned to Srinagar, where he died, and where his tomb and shrine receive veneration. Ramanuja claimed to be eighth in succession from Naum'arwar, and founded a special church or *sampradaya*. But the essential point about him is his

9 Quoted in Otto, *Mysticism, East and West*. Chapter V.

intense opposition to the teaching handed down from Sankara. He is really indignant about it, and says:

> 'This entire teaching . . . is nothing but a web of false reasoning, scoffing at every logical distinction. . . . His (Sankara's) understanding must have been disturbed by illusory imaginations, arising from the sins he has committed in his previous births. . . . He who knows the right relation of things, as they appear in passages of the Scriptures logically taken, as they are given in perception, and as they arise from all other sources or knowledge, must reject such foolish doctrines.'

Against the *Kevala advaita*, Ramanuja sets out his own theistic doctrine, which is remarkably close to that of Christian theology, but yet differs from it in certain vital particulars. Thus, although he affirms the absolute reality of the world, he does not conceive it as being led towards perfection as a goal, but simply as created, sustained, and dissolved by God. It exists only to pass away repeatedly, and to rise again in endless repetition. It is never transfigured. It is the *lila*, sport, or surplus energy of God, and not necessary to Him for His self-realisation; nor does He sacrifice Himself to redeem it.

Ramanuja, like Sankara, wrote commentaries on the Upanishads, but always in the interest of their interpretation in terms of his own doctrine of qualified duality, or *vishtadvaita*, as it is called. He thus gave an intellectual basis to the movement in both Saivism and Vaishnavism which stressed the partial separateness of the soul from God, and the affectionate relationship persisting between God and the soul. A later teacher, Madhva (1199), carried the doctrine still further in the direction of a complete duality between the soul and God (*dvaita*), whereas Ramanuja had been inclined to consider what has been called 'panentheism' as the final state of the soul. It is curious to notice that Ramanuja's followers have become divided into two schools over the question of the operation of Divine Grace. The northern, or Vadagalais, stress the freedom of the will, and say that the soul lays hold of God (this corresponds in Christian theology to the doctrine of synergism or co-operation, as taught by St. John Cassian). The southern, or Tengalais, stress the priority of God and the necessary prevenience of grace (after the manner of St. Augustine the Great). It is this difference that has caused them to be called respectively the monkey and cat schools of theology, since the young monkey holds on to its mother in order to be carried, whereas the kitten is picked up by its mother with her jaws.

After Ramanuja and Madhva, the next teacher of importance is Ramanand. Indian tradition gives the date of his birth as 1299, but it seems to Eliot more likely that he flourished about the year 1400. If so, he verges upon the period when Islam had already begun to exercise considerable influence upon Indian religion. To the Moslem incursions, then, we must turn in the next chapter.

Another most important figure about this time is Jñānesvar, whose chief work, the Jñānesvari, was completed in the year 1290. His influence, according to one Hindu authority of great weight, has been greater than that of any other Maratha saint except Tukārām (see next chapter) and he is one of the first to compose large numbers of *bhakti* hymns. A typical one may here be given:[10]

> To the dwelling of the saints take thy way;
> There the Lord himself shall not say thee nay.
>
> Cry Ramkrishna—tis the path of life's goal.
> Worship Rama—he who is Vishnu's soul.
>
> Him whose name is unity, whoso find,
> Fetters of duality cannot bind.
>
> All the lustre and the glow Yogis gain,
> By this name honeysweet we attain.
>
> On Pralhada's childish lips dwelt the name
> While to Uddhav bringing gifts Krishna came.[11]
>
> Easy 'tis to utter it: Is't not true?
> Yet who use it anywhere, Ah, how few.

The Maratha literary renaissance, as it has been called, extends from the thirteenth to the seventeenth century, and produces an abundance of lyric poetry of a high quality, much of which is religious. Jñānesvar's two brothers and his sister were also reputed to have been poets, and in the next chapter we shall tell of other later rhapsodists, whose work gained inspiration partly from the theistic reaction of the middle ages, partly from the infusion of new religious ideas by Moslem missionaries.

The resemblances between this literature and that of medieval Christian Europe have often been pointed out. Thus the following hymn of Jñānesvar's reads like a composition by St. Bernard of Clairvaux.

10 The translations are from Dr. Nicol MacNicol's *Psalms of Maratha Saints.*
11 Pralhada and Uddhav were famous Vaishnava devotees

There needs not a propitious hour
    This Name to cry,
Lo, both who speak it and who hears
    Are saved thereby.

This holy Name bears quite away
    All man's offence—
Hari, the saviour e'en of men
    Of little sense.

Who speaks this Name, the soul of all,
    O happy they
Plain for their Father's feet they make
    The heavenward way.

But the resemblance is perhaps only superficial, since the deity so addressed is a more or less mythical being called Vithoba, who is worshipped as an *avatar* of Vishnu at the sanctuary of Pandharpur.

Meanwhile we may sum up the survey of this period by drawing attention to two further points:

The effect of bhakti on the valuation of caste: Neither Sankara nor Ramanuja actually advocated its abolition; but the kind of free devotion which they encouraged weakened its religious aspect. The Brahmin system continued as part of the social order, but anyone, it was held, who displayed the necessary earnestness could have immediate access to God, and needed neither priest nor ritual sacrifice. It is noticeable that at Puri, the famous temple of Jagannath, which is now a Vaishnavite centre, there is a rule which waives the operation of caste distinctions within the precincts of the sanctuary.

The rise of the later sectarian literature: This includes the Puranas, the Tantras, and vast quantities of vernacular hymns.

The word *Purana* means 'an ancient story which ought to be learnt', and the literature which bears this name probably began at the time of the Gupta dynasty, or a century earlier. Alberuni mentions the existence of eighteen Puranas about A.D. 1030, but the number is actually greater. The most influential and widely read is the eighth or ninth century A.D., and is concerned with stories about the youth of Krishna, the alleged *avator* of Vishnu. There is a free translation into Hindi of the tenth book, called the *Prem Sagar*, or Ocean of Love, which is greatly revered in North India. This and other Puranas are frequently read aloud at temple services, but the quality of their contents falls generally below the level of that of the main Vedic and Upanishadic literature. The stories which they contain are often fantastic and sometimes obscene. The Tantras are virtually manuals and prescriptions of religious ritual and magic, and are chiefly connected with the worship of the female principle in nature.

This later literature is something of an embarrassment to educated and enlightened Hindus, who are conscious that it is of a very different order from that of the bulk of the Upanishads, and from the commentaries made upon them by such saintly souls as Sankara and Ramanuja. The same problem to a less extent has, of course, presented itself to Christians when they are faced with the apocryphal gospels, or with medieval legends of saints, or with monastic commentaries of a quality much inferior to that of the best patristic or modern theological literature. But whereas Christians have exercised a rather severe discrimination between canonical and non-canonical books, the division into *śruti* and *smriti* has hardly had the same effect, since a good deal of the *smriti* is of a noble character (e.g., Ramayana and the Gita) and hardly deserves to be lumped together with the Puranas, while the Christian canon does at any rate exclude the foolish and extravagant legendary tales of the childhood of Jesus.[12]

BOOKS FOR FURTHER STUDY

RUDOLF OTTO. *Mysticism East and West*. Macmillans. 1932. *India's Religion of Grace*. Student Movement Press. 1930.

JOSEPH ESTLIN CARPENTER. *Theism in Medieval India*. London. 1921.

BHARATAN KUMARAPPA. *The Hindu Conception of Deity as culminating in Ramanuja*. London University Press. 1934.

NICOL MACNICOL. *Psalms of the Maratha Saints*. Calcutta. 1919. *Indian Theism*. Oxford. 1915.

12 Professor Dasgupta has kindly furnished me with an important reference at this point, from the *Mimamsa Sutra*, the terms of which are as follows:

'When a *smriti* is found to be in conflict with a *śruti*, the *smriti* is to be regarded as cancelled; but if the statement in the *smriti* is not directly antagonistic to the *śruti*, we may surmise that probably there was a *śruti* to the same effect, but that it has now been lost.'

This canon, as will be seen, exempts Hindus from any obligation to observe any of the pious practices such as cow-worship, etc., which are not expressly enjoined by the *śruti*, and with which the early Vedic literature can actually be shown to be in conflict. But it does not say anything about the rather free or allegorical interpretation of the *śruti* which would be necessary if some of the items contained in them were not to be held binding upon the modern Indian.

7

ISLAM IN INDIA AND ITS CONSEQUENCES
LATER BHAKTI. SAKTISM

No record of Hinduism can be fair which leaves out of account the influence of Islam.

Mohammed died in A.D. 632, and within a hundred years the Arabs had carried their expansions as far as the Pyrenees in the West, entering Spain in 711, and France in 732, and being driven out again by Charles Martel. At almost exactly the same time, 712, they invaded India and occupied Sind, its most westerly area, which is separated from the rest of the country by a great belt of desert. There they stopped, either because at that time India was strong enough to resist them or because campaigning across the desert was unattractive. Sind soon fell away from the central government of Baghdad, and became independent. Meanwhile peaceful cultural intercourse sprang up between both North and South India and the Abbasid capital, and this meant that Indians first became acquainted with Islam as a religion producing a specific culture. Moslem missionaries soon after entered the Hindu states; and Hinduism, with its characteristic tolerance, allowed them to make converts if they were able, and to build mosques. On the whole, India learnt less at first from the Moslems than they learnt from her. Indian mathematics, astronomy, and medicine were eagerly studied at Baghdad, but those who taught them remained somewhat aloof from the vigorous intellectual life of that wonderful city. Gradually the Moslem Abbasid Empire weakened and split up, and the power in Central Asia and Mesopotamia passed to the Seljuk Turks. One of these, Sultan Mahmud of Ghazni, established himself in Afghanistan, and thence, about A.D. 100, made a series of rather ruthless plundering expeditions into North India. In Kashmir and Rajputana he met with defeat, but he conquered and annexed Sind and the Punjab, and then returned to Ghazni. He was not a religious leader, and he actually made use of a Hindu as one of his generals against his own Moslem rivals, and deported large numbers of Hindu artisans into his own dominions. This was the age when Alberuni,[1] the Persian traveller from Kniva, visited India and wrote down his impressions. He suggests that the Hindu leaders of that day were self-satisfied, haughty, and therefore not accessible to new ideas, and the success of Mahmud's raids indicates the probability that decay was beginning to set in throughout the life of North India, though the South apparently continued for some centuries to be extremely vigorous. Mahmud died in 1030, and no further extension of Moslem rule beyond the Punjab took place for the next 160 years. Then an Afghan, Shahab-ud-Din Ghuri, captured Ghazni, overthrew the existing government, and invaded India as far as Delhi. The king of the latter city defeated him on his first attack, but a year later Shahab returned, captured Delhi, and made himself sovereign of it.

This did not mean the conquest of the South of India, but it meant that a large part of the North passed under Afghan rule. The Afghans are defined as Indo-Aryan in race, and not Turks. Although they had accepted Islam, they were, in fact, closely related in physical descent to the peoples of North-West India. Some have compared them to the Danes or to the Nordic Prussian military aristocracy. They were mountaineers, hard and uncultured, and they ruled their Indian sub-jects with brutal strength, though they intermarried with Hindu women, and softened gradually in their ways. They extended their power by stages further south, though not so far as to conquer the great and flourishing states of Pandya and Vijayanagar. Then, later in the fourteenth century, there came the terrible raid by the Turco-Mongol, Timour. He was only a few months in North India, but he slaughtered the inhabitants with such ferocity that along his route lay pyramids of skulls from the corpses of his victims; and he left Delhi a deserted wreck. It took many years for the city to recover, and in the meantime the Indo-Afghan Empire in North India had split up into a number of independent states. In 1526 there came another Turco-Mongol invader, Babar, a prince of the same dynasty as Timour. He also took Delhi, and with him began a new regime, that of the Mughal Empire, which lasted until the British conquest in 1757. Babar's success is said to have been due to his use of artillery. The line

1 See p. 87.

of Emperors which he founded endured for about 200 years, and then between 1707 and 1818 its power fell to pieces, and was replaced by British domination.

This brief survey of political events must serve to give the necessary background to the history of the fortunes of Hinduism during the same period. Nehru insists that in the strict sense of the word there was no *Moslem* invasion, nor has there been a *Moslem* period in the history of India, any more than the British invasion was a *Christian* invasion, or the period of British rule a *Christian* period.[2] It does not follow that everyone will agree with him, but it is certainly the case that the invaders merged themselves into Indian life to a remarkable degree. This is less surprising in the case of the Afghans, who were at any rate (so to speak) cousins of the high-caste Hindus, but the Turks were Mongols, yet in the case of the later Sultans of Delhi, two had Hindu mothers, and in the South the Moslem ruler of Gulbarga married a Hindu princess of Vijayanagar, though such marriages were not common.

There was in fact quite a fair degree of mutual influence between Hindus and Moslems, and this manifested itself in the production of a mixed culture. Although Persian became the language of polite society, many Moslems learnt to use Hindi, and one, Amir Khusran, a Turk of the United Provinces, made himself famous for his popular songs, and riddles for children, which have persisted in all classes for 600 years. Conversions from Hinduism to Islam, except in the upper classes, went by castes or groups. The result of this has been to mix up Hindus and Moslems in many districts. Certain occupations have tended to become monopolised by Moslems. Thus in large areas they are mostly the weavers. In others they are the butchers or the shoe-merchants. Tailors are almost always Moslems.

One of the marked later developments which took place was that of *purdah* or the seclusion of women among the Hindus. This grew in India in Mughal times, and seems to have been associated with high rank among both Hindus and Moslems; but in the South it has not prevailed, and curiously enough, it is not strong just where we should have expected to find it, namely in the Punjab or the Frontier Province, although these are predominantly Moslem districts.

During the fifteenth century there was a genuine attempt to encourage a synthesis between the religions of the conquerors and the conquered, and new ideas began to stir in people's minds. Some folk left North India, and trekked south to get away from foreign influence,

2 *See* Nehru, op. cit. p. 198

and the South thus became a stronghold of Hindu orthodoxy. But others almost insensibly adjusted themselves to new ways, though these were chiefly members of the nobility and upper classes, the rural peasant populations remaining relatively unaffected. At this time there arose a new set of reformers, who preached a compromise between Hinduism and Islam, and either ignored or denounced the caste system.[3]

Such was Ramanand, who, though a southerner, travelled north and made an important disciple in the person of Kabir, a Moslem weaver of Benares. Ramanand himself was a Vaishnavite with a special devotion to the Rama *avatar*. With him and with Kabir, *bhakti* enters upon a new phase. The point about Rama is that his relation to the soul has not the same erotic associations as that of Krishna, and that when divested of mythical accretions he appears as a pure and lofty type of *avatar* capable of playing a part in a blend of Hinduism and Islam. Ramanand gathered to him twelve disciples, one of whom was a raja, while another was a leatherseller, and therefore an outcaste or untouchable, and a third was Kabir. Others were Brahmans. This new movement, called the Ramat, had a profound effect on the popular literature of India during the fifteenth and sixteenth centuries. In the South the vernacular had been used for some time for the composition of hymns, but now Ramanand gave authority for its use in a similar fashion in the North, where so far Sanskrit had been regarded as the only proper language to employ in religious worship.

The situation recalls that which prevailed in Europe at the time when Luther and his companions began to issue hymns in the vernacular, and when it was said by a Papal official that the people had sung themselves into heresy. A great stream of religious lyrics now pours forth. One branch of it is Krishnaite, another is Ramaite, and a third is associated with those who, like Kabir, avowedly sought to create a new religion out of a combination of Hindu and Moslem elements. Almost every locality makes its contribution. About 1420 we have the poems of Mira Bai, the Krishnaite devotee, wife of the Raja of Chitore, whose erotic ecstasies according to one legend culminated in a miracle in which the image of Krishna came to life and descended from his pedestal to embrace her. Two Bengali poets, Vidyapati and Chandi Das, were her contemporaries, and the hymns they wrote form one of the principal sacred books of the Bengali Vaishnavas. Vallabha, who was born in 1470, was a Brahmin who settled at Benares, and had a special devotion to the infant Krishna. He also wrote sacred poems, and his theology verges upon monism, and is

3 *See* J. Estlin Carpenter: *Theism in Medieval India.*

less theistic than is usual among Vaishnavas. Vallabha's pantheistic tendencies have led the sect which he founded into regrettable antinomian licentiousness, and in 1780 a protest against them was made by another Vaishnavite Brahmin, Swami Narayana, who founded a temple and a large monastery at Ahmedabad. There are still about 200,000 of this sect, with a celibate clergy, and a community of about 300 monks.

Another Krishnaite revivalist was Chaitanya, who was born in 1485 at Nadia. In his sect caste was not observed, and many Moslems are said to have been admitted as members. Possibly the practices of dervishes may have been linked up in some way with the devotional exercises of Chaitanya's disciples, as the ones he especially enjoined included chanting of the Divine Names accompanied by music and dancing, and the swaying of the body. Hymns called *kirtans* are sung, and *bhajans* or song-services continue for hours at a time. The whole affair is reminiscent of revival meetings in Wales or among negroes in the Southern States of America. Chaitanya maintained that salvation was to be obtained solely by *bhakti* or devotion,—self-surrender without hoping for any reward. 'He who expects remuneration for his love acts as a trader.' In this *bhakti* there are five degrees:

  (i) *santi*, or calm meditation;
  (ii) *dasya*, or servitude;
  (iii) *sakhya*, or friendship;
  (iv) *vatsakya*, love like that of a child for its parent;
  (v) *madhurya*, or love like that of a woman for her lover.

The name by which God is chiefly known in this *bhakti* is *Hari*, which is popularly interpreted as meaning 'the One who removes sin'.

In the preceding chapter we referred to the development of Vaishnavite poet-saints in the Maratha country. This succession continues right up to the close of the seventeenth century, and the three most important in this later period are Namdev, who is probably to be dated about 1400, Tukārām (1608–1649), and Ram Das, all of whom composed hymns of great beauty and deep religious feeling. Namdev declared that fasting, austerities, and pilgrimages were unnecessary. All that mattered was 'to hold fast to the love of Hari's name'.

The following is by Namdev:

> Now all my days with joy I'll fill, full to the brim,
> With all my heart to Vitthal cling, and only him.
>
> He will sweep utterly away all dole and care;
> And all in sunder shall I rend illusion's snare.

O altogether dear is He and He alone,
For all my burden He will take to be his own.

Lo all the sorrow of the world will straightway cease,
And all unending now shall be the reign of peace.

And here is a similar work by Tukārām:

God is ours, yea, ours is He,
Soul of all the souls that be.

God is nigh without a doubt,
Nigh to all, within, without.

God is gracious, gracious still;
Every longing he'll fulfil.

God protects, protects His own;
Strife and death He casteth down.

Kind is God, ah, kind indeed;
Tuka he will guide and lead.'

It is difficult to fathom the real beliefs of these earnest men. The translations of their poems are, of course, made by Christians,[4] and words
which occur in them have a Christian connotation, and their Marathi
counterparts may not bear quite the same meaning. That the composers
were not idolaters in the ordinary sense is clear, and this may be due
to Moslem influence. Thus Tukārām wrote:

A stone with red lead painted o'er
Brats and women bow before.

This couplet might almost be Bishop Heber's. Namdev expresses
himself still more explicitly: 'No *guru* can show me God: wherever I
go there are stone gods painted red. How can a stone god speak? When
will he ever utter speech? My mind is weary of those who say, God,
God. Everywhere I go they say, Worship a stone. He is God whom
Nama holds in his heart. Nama will never forsake the feet of Krishna.'
The Hindu psalmists, however, are almost entirely conscious of
Deity as 'a pervading Presence in nature, without clearly defined moral
characteristics'. The spirit of the fifteenth of the Hebrew canonical

4 In these cases by Dr. MacNicol.

psalms is mostly absent. For these mystics the ideal man is one who has reached a haven of tranquillity:

> No wind of good or ill shall enter there
> But peace supremely still, supremely fair.

'They have no vision of a world judged or a world redeemed, for their god is their own personal god—not the nation's or the world's.' Such a description might, of course, be applied to some of the doctrine in the hymns by Moody and Sankey. Occasionally Tukārām displays a sense of compassion for others, but, as MacNicol says, this is a rare mood, and seldom finds expression in his poems. Equally, however, he never displays the wrath and indignation of the Hebrew. There is nothing to correspond to the passage: 'Do not I hate them O Lord that hate Thee? Yea, I hate them right sore, even as though they were mine enemies.' The reason for this is not far to seek. However theistic the psalmists of India may seem to be there is always the background of Advaita, so that Muktabai in the thirteenth century writes:

> Thou pervading Brahman art
> How should anger fill thy heart?

Yet in justice it must be said that the *bhakti* saints do occasionally give utterance to precepts which have almost a flavour of moral Hebrew prophetism: Thus Tukārām says in one place:

> He whose words and acts agree
> Let his footsteps praised be.

In Assam the most notable revivalists were Sankar Deb, in the sixteenth century, and his successor Mahdab Deb, whose writings are treated as Holy Scripture by his followers. This branch of Vaishnavism recognises caste and is more under Brahmin control.

Tulsi Das, who was born in 1532, stands in a class by himself. At the age of forty-three he began in Oudh to write a new version of the Ramayana, and completed it at Benares where he died in 1623. His Ramayana is treated in the North-West Provinces with at least as much esteem as the Bible in England, and it is indeed a remarkable work. It is no slavish translation of Valmiki, but an original poem, in which the story of Rama is re-told with much enrichment, and with an immensely increased emphasis upon the *avatar*-motif. Rama, who, in the original epic, is entirely human, in the hands of Tulsi Das becomes invested with all kinds of miraculous powers and attributes, and is as much like the incarnate Logos as any figure in Indian theology. An English version of one quatrain may be quoted:

> Seers and sages, saints and hermits, fix on him their reverent gaze,
> And in faint and trembling accents, holy scripture hymns his praise.
> He, the omnipresent spirit, lord of heaven and earth and hell,
> To redeem his people, freely has vouchsafed with men to dwell.

No Christmas carol could be more explicitly orthodox.[5]

Sir George Grierson has said that Tulsi Das was the first Hindu to declare that God was able to sympathise with our infirmities, and since this is a specifically Christian doctrine, he thinks that traces of the influence of Nestorian Christianity can be discerned here. Although Grierson enumerates thirteen other poets who composed Ramayanas in some dialect of Hindi, Tulsi was the most famous of all. He was a great exponent of *bhakti*, and his saying is often quoted: 'the worship of the Impersonal laid no hold upon my heart'. Yet he is still characteristically Hindu, since, although he holds that supreme bliss consists in the reciprocal relations of God and the soul, he often, though no doubt inconsistently, uses the language of *advaita*. Rama is Deity, the totality of good, imperishable, invisible, uncreated, incomparable, void of all change, indivisible, whom the Vedas declare that they cannot define. By the power of Rama, Brahma, Vishnu, and Siva exist (apparently as inferior beings). Deity is called 'the annihilator of duality'.

When we come to Kabir and his associates we find ourselves on very different ground. His exact date is not known, but we may place him in the middle of the fifteenth century. As has already been said, he is believed to have been born and brought up as a Moslem at Benares, but he became a disciple of Ramanand, and henceforth stands between the two religions, with a slight bias towards Hinduism which increased in his followers. Numerous hymns and aphorisms are attributed to him, some possibly not authentic. He puts Hindus and Moslems on the same footing, and says 'Kabir is a child of Allah and Ram'. He condemns caste, circumcision, and idolatry, and rejects the idea of *avatars*. Yet his theology in other respects is Hindu rather than Moslem, and he refers to 'the cosmic illusion', to transmigration, and to the sanctity of all life, even in plants. A flower-girl is upbraided for cutting leaves, because 'in every leaf there is life'. Salvation, as in Buddhism, means release from *samsara*, and identification of the soul

5 Or even Apollinarian!

with Deity. Yet Kabir hovers on the brink of theism. Through Islam he can unconsciously be touched by Judaism and Christianity. He has a strong sense of sin, and in one memorable phrase he says: 'My Father is the Great Lord of the earth; to that Father how shall I go?'

Kabir's liberalism is shown in the following:

'If God dwell only in the mosque, to whom belongeth the rest of the country? They who are called Hindus say that God dwelleth in an idol: I see not the truth in either sect.'

One of his poems runs as follows:

'The name of God is my wealth;
I cannot tie it in a knot; or sell it for my livelihood.
The Name is my field, the Name is my garden.
I Thy slave, O God, perform Thy service and seek Thy protection.
Thy Name is my wealth, Thy Name my capital;
I know none but Thee.
Thy Name is my kindred, Thy Name my brethren.
Thy Name my associates who will assist me at the last moment.'

There is still a community of about a million adherents which reveres Kabir as a teacher, and preserves scriptures known as the Kabirpanth. There are also a few smaller sects which acknowledge his influence, the Satnamis, founded in 1750, who are almost ordinary Hindus; the Radhaswamis (1561), who profess to have developed along Christian lines; and the Dadupanthis (1603), a more or less male community with a strong interest in military service, who recruit their members by adopting boys whom they train for the army.

The Sikh religion can hardly be ignored in this chapter, although it cannot strictly be regarded as a part of Hinduism. The founder, Nanak (1469–1538), was a Hindu from near Lahore, who came under Moslem influence, and, like Kabir, conceived the idea of uniting the two religions. Like Kabir, he has left prose and lyric writing, and though of the two he has more Hindu allusions, in spirit he is more Moslem. He gathered a sect and named as his successor or *guru* one Angada. The word 'Sikh' simply means 'disciple'. Sikhs have the peculiarity of being, like the Moslem Senussi of North Africa, a sort of political as well as religious community, with a distinct costume and social customs. Their sacred book is called the Granth, and includes not only hymns by the founder and the *gurus* who succeeded him, but also hymns by Kabir and by some of the medieval Hindu *bhagats* or saints, such as Namdev, Ramanand, and Jaidev. The most famous temple of the Sikhs is at Amritsar, and is known as the Golden Temple. It is not the original structure, since the latter was destroyed by fire, and has been rebuilt.

Akbar, the Mughal reigning at Delhi in the middle of the sixteenth century, was a remarkably tolerant sovereign, and under him the Sikhs were encouraged. He himself in 1579 abandoned orthodox Islam, and adopted some Hindu observances, and later still he endeavoured to fashion a new synthetic religion, with elements drawn from Hinduism, Islam, Judaism, Christianity, and Zoroastrianism. It is not quite certain how much of this was vanity, and how much sincere piety and desire for comprehensive unity, since Akbar's *Din-I-Ilahi* or 'Divine Faith' seems to have recognised him as God's vice-regent, even if not actually himself God incarnate, and he appears to have countenanced the forgery of a document known as the 'Allah Upanishad', which was claimed as an authentic part of the old Atharva Veda, and most conveniently identifies the Allah of 'the Prophet Mohammed Akbar' with Mitra, Varuna, Indra, etc. Akbar's new creed did not long survive his decease, and the only consequence which concerns us here is that it led one of his successors to cause a Persian translation of the genuine Upanishads to be made. This is the one referred to on page 47.

It may perhaps be a matter of surprise that when the British arrived in India they formed on the whole such an unfavourable estimate of Hinduism, if all that has been described in this chapter is true.

The fact is that Hinduism in its very long history has gone through phases of debasement, and one of its worst periods coincided with the advent of the British in the middle of the eighteenth century, when the spiritual movements of the sixteenth and seventeenth centuries had spent their force. But it is also true to say that Hinduism, being an ethnic rather than a prophetic or 'founded' religion, is a jungle of mixed growths, and some of these are very rank, not to say evil, even as judged by Hindu standards. Thus Saktism, or the worship of the female principle in nature, personified by the spouse of Siva, is accompanied in places by the darkest and most obscene rites, surviving perhaps from the depths of past aboriginal populations, and sometimes associated with human sacrifice, which was certainly, up till comparatively recent times, offered at the grim temple of Kamakhya on the banks of the Brahmaputra. In the main, Saktism flourishes in North-East India, among populations largely non-Aryan, and most respectable Hindus condemn both it and its sacred scriptures or Tantras. It is probably this worship of sexuality which has given Hinduism a bad name, and until it can be suppressed by Indians themselves it must continue to be a blot upon the national life, though its prevalence has been most unjustly exaggerated by superficial writers about India. The manifestation of Siva's Sakti in the forms of Durga or Kali is accompanied by such grotesque ceremonies as those of the Kalighat at Calcutta, where Eliot says educated Hindus may still be seen cutting the throats of goats before the repulsive and monstrous image of Kali. But it is not quite certain how far Eliot is just at this point.[6] C. F. Andrews, writing in 1939, described this relic of animal sacrifice as clearly moribund, catering merely for the ignorant and superstitious among the lowest ranks of the huge population of the metropolis. He points out that Hinduism in the majority of its places of worship has abandoned animal sacrifice altogether, and substituted for it the beautiful custom of offering flowers. Still he admits that it is altogether inexcusable that a united storm of protest from the whole educated community has not long ago been raised against the continuance of unpleasant customs, and he sees in this a sign of moral weakness, a lack of moral fibre in those who are leaders of public opinion, which needs to be taken account of by everyone in India who sets out to be a reformer. This judgment on the part of one who is known to have been a warm friend of the Indian people, and who was in his lifetime both

6 A very different picture of the cult of Kali was given recently by a soldier serving in India. He happened to be in Delhi at the time of the Festival of Lights—Dewali. The whole of the Hindu quarter was wonderfully illuminated, and vast masses of little statuettes of the goddess were on sale. He went to see a small temple dedicated to Kali, and on his arrival he found that the offerings consisted of fruit and flowers. A priest who spoke to him in English gave him some of the fruit which had been received in sacrifice, and explained that it was a token of goodwill from the goddess. The actual words spoken may be quoted in full:

'Kali is the goddess of creation and fertility. She carries a scimitar because destruction and creation go hand in hand. Hindus worship the meaning of Kali, not the image, and that meaning is the creative vibration by which everything comes into being. No Hindu is an *idol*-worshipper. Where Christians say: In the beginning was the Word, Hindus say: In the beginning was Kali, the Life-Force.'

It must be evident that here reforming influences are seen penetrating into popular religion; but to what extent the masses of the peasantry really hold this belief about Kali as the personification of *l'élan vital* it is difficult to judge. Naturally it would be instinctive in an educated priest to give the most favourable account that he could of the institution which he served. As the temple is described as a small one, it seems not unlikely that it was another example of a modernising venture, and this may account for the fact that the soldier was invited to go and see it. This would be propaganda on the part of liberal Hindus. The hypothesis is strengthened by his observation that attached to the temple was a marquee where men and women were singing hymns to the accompaniment of a harmonium. This would no doubt be a sort of *kirtan*, or *bhajan*, but it sounds very unlike the ordinary methods, wherein native drums are employed to give the accompaniment.

loved and respected by them, is noteworthy. But there is good hope that such debasing anachronisms, as Andrews calls them, will now cease by the will of the Indian people themselves, and it must be pointed out that the liberal Hindu, Tagore, of whom we shall speak in the next chapter, wrote a play in denunciation of the ceremonies at Kalighat, which is acted openly in Calcutta, and has also been filmed, yet without any riot or other hostile reaction. The younger Hindu nationalists point out that it is worth giving India a chance to regenerate herself, and that she is less likely to do so as long as she does not feel personal responsibility for the task.

BOOKS FOR FURTHER STUDY

M. T. TITUS. *Islam in India*. Oxford. 1930.

M. A. MCAULIFFE. *The Sikh Religion*. Six vols. Oxford. 1909.

NICOL MACNICOL. op. cit.

8

THE BRITISH OCCUPATION AND ITS EFFECTS

REFORMING MOVEMENTS AND PERSONALITIES

It will be best to begin this chapter by limiting the field.

(1) We are not concerned with any political questions. The story of Britain's part in the history of India may be related from the point of view of an imperialist, a liberal, or a Hindu nationalist either of the type of Tagore, Gandhi, or Nehru. But it cannot be told here.

(2) We are not concerned with the success or non-success of Christian missions, or with any claim of superiority that Christianity may make over Hinduism.

This book aims at giving a true and scientific account of Hinduism itself, and therefore it must only be concerned with objectively recording any religious effects which can be seen to have accrued from the British domination of India. Let these then be stated as briefly as possible.

We may discern two stages, the first, one of de-nationalisation and to some extent of westernisation; the seond, one of nationalism and of reform. Stage one begins naturally with the reaction of the Christians who entered India to what they saw there. They found, in the first place, to quote the words of Nehru:[1] 'an Asia which had become dormant, exhausted as it were, by its past efforts'. . . . 'The dynamic quality which was becoming evident in Europe was almost wholly absent in India.' There was 'a paralysis of creative energy' and 'petrifaction'. They saw and felt all this, and whether rightly or wrongly, it gave them a feeling of superiority, which Indians were quick to

[1] Op. cit. pp. 182–3 and 216–17.

detect. Further, they found a religion which in certain respects *differed* very greatly from theirs. Whether, like Abbé Dubois, they were Roman Catholics, or, like Ziegenbalg Schwartz, Carey, Marshman, and Henry Martyn, they were Protestants, they were conscious of this difference. It must not be supposed that they necessarily felt that the Hinduism they observed was in every respect *inferior* to Christianity. No doubt in its more degraded forms it may have seemed so, and Abbé Dubois, Catholic as he was, was impressed by the extravagant amount of ceremonial customs connected with Brahmanism, though he also noted the presence of ascetics, philosophers, and mystics who could compare with many to be found in Christian countries. The Ramayana was rendered into Italian by Goressio in 1843, and into English by the Baptist missionaries Carey and Marshman in 1806, and its evident merits were thus recognised; while, as we have already seen, the Upanishads began to be known in Europe about the same time. But there were two great points of difference between Indian and European religion. First, there was a *lack of the moral background provided by the ethical teachings of the Old and New Testaments*, and the Supreme Being of the Hindus was 'beyond good and evil'. Second, there was *not the same insistence upon the importance of historical events as in the Christian creed and gospels.*

For some time there was a tendency on the part of intelligent Indians to accept the liberal ideas of Europe with enthusiasm, and this was well expressed in a retrospective survey made by Rabindranath Tagore in 1941 on his eightieth birthday, only a few months before his death. It is a mistake to regard the rising of 1857 as mainly nationalist. It was largely a revolt of feudal elements, and it was actually suppressed with the aid of Indian support. At the same time, as Sir Thomas Munro saw as early as 1817, it was due to a faulty method of government, which eventually provoked a widespread outburst of anti-foreign sentiment.

With the middle of the nineteenth century, however, began a series of reforming movements, some of them compromises between Hinduism and Christianity, others attempts at the rejuvenation of Hinduism itself. Indians could not fail to be impressed by the valuation set by Christians upon their Bible, and this stimulated them to a fresh study of their own heritage, and to a more earnest valuation of its contents. Moreover, the persistent education of Hindus in European languages and literature, and their visits to foreign centres of education, were bound to exercise a disturbing influence upon their traditional orthodoxy, and made a good many of them adopt an ill-mixed amal-

gam of Indian and European ideas and jargon.[2] But this phase was merely
a transitional one of intellectual adolescence, and was bound to endure
only until Indians were able to acquire enough grip of the new learning
to enable them to apply it to the renewal of their national life and
literature from within.

The first and most natural effect of this sudden impact of Europe
upon India was to be seen in the alteration of the balance between the
affirmation and rejection of life in this world. This is well illustrated
in the teachings of the various reforming Hindus with whom we shall
shortly be concerned. As Schweitzer has put it:[3] 'These men undertook
more energetically than any of their predecessors to combine with the
ethic of becoming more perfect in heart the ethic which seeks activity
within the world.' But it must be duly recognised that this combination was also influencing the Christianity of Europe. Prior to the
beginning of the nineteenth century there had been for a long time
comparatively little interest on the part of Christians in anything more
than what has been called ambulance work on behalf of humanity.
Secular movements such as utilitarianism, Chartism, and early Marxism
stimulated Christians to a re-exploration of the social implications of
their belief, and it was this newer Christianity, with its practical expression in various phases of missionary and social activity, which
influenced so strongly the earnest men and women of India. The change
that was wrought is well put by C. F. Andrews, writing in 1908.[4] He
says: 'One thing is apparent in educated India today. There is *life* where
before there was stagnation. The spiritual nature of Indian thinkers and
writers is absorbed in the prospect of an awakening East, an Indian
nation, a free and enlightened people, a deliverance from the night-
mare of superstition and the tyranny of caste. . . . Young India is
wakeful, alert, precocious; it turns to its national leaders as to a magnet,
and is irresistibly attracted.' This movement was essentially Hindu
rather than Moslem, since Moslems have had their own approach to
the problems of the modern world, and that is another story, which
cannot be told here. What we have to study are the steps by which
the situation described by Andrews came into existence.

Andrews says that at first the Indians, conscious of their own weak-

2 It is no discredit to Indians that they have had to go through this stage of transition. The same process is to be observed at the present time in West Africa, where gifted
young Africans are struggling to express a valuation of their own cultural heritage in
books written in English. A notable example of this is to be seen in Mr. Danquah's work
on the African conception of God.

3 *Indian Thought and its Development*, p. 209.

4 In *North India*, S.P.G. Handbooks, and *The Renaissance in India* chapters iv and v.

ness, were rather overwhelmed by the strength of the Western world. To learn English, to read English literature, to follow English manners, was for a time the prevailing fashion, and the education that was given fostered this fashion to the utmost. It is true that some of the missionaries, at least indirectly, encouraged a return to native interests by their translations of Christian works into the vernacular of the greater Indian languages, by the rendering of Hindu classics into English,[5] and by reducing the lesser languages and dialects to a literary form. It was they, indeed, who set up the first private printing presses, and against considerable government opposition encouraged the spread of vernacular printed literature, and promoted the growth of literacy. Still, the first stage was nevertheless a westernising one.

Then the tide began to turn; and it will be best to link up this second stage with the personalities of the reformers whom it produced.

The first name which we encounter is that of Raja Ram Mohan Roy, who was born as far back as 1772. A gifted Bengali Brahmin of Vaishnava parentage, he was brought up in a mixed Hindu-Moslem culture. As a boy he read the Puranas, and soon rebelled against their myths and fairy tales. (It is significant that this always seems to be the point at which Hindu reformers break away from tradition. Clearly they feel that in the literature and practices of later sectarian Hinduism there is something of which they ought rightly to be ashamed.)

At the age of sixteen Ram Mohan Roy composed a tract against idolatry, partly inspired by Moslem and Christian influences, but partly also by a study of the Vedas and the Upanishads. Nehru speaks of him as a 'towering personality' with a 'curious and adventurous mind', and Monier-Williams has described him as perhaps the first earnest-minded investigator in the science of Comparative Religion that the world has produced. In order to study the sources of Western culture he learnt English, Greek, Latin, and Hebrew, and after visiting Benares and Tibet he also learnt Arabic in order to read the Qu'rān. After his father's death in 1803 he entered more openly into controversy with orthodox Hindus, and during the ensuing twenty years he inclined more and more in the direction of Christianity, so that in 1820 he actually published a book entitled *The Precepts of Jesus* in Bengali and English. In 1828 (although hitherto he had kept outside any denomination) he began to attend a Unitarian chapel in Calcutta, and eventually established a conventicle of his own, and composed a form for public worship. This latter was a new feature in Hinduism, and the sect so

5 Cf. the series of books edited by Dr. J. N. Farquhar, entitled *The Heritage of India*.

formed was called the 'Brahmo-Samaj' or 'Society of Believers in One Self-Existent Deity'. There was no suggestion on the part of the founder that he thought himself to be inventing a new religion. What he wished was to establish an institution where Hindus, Moslems, Christians, Parsees, and indeed any others who felt so inclined, could assemble themselves together for common prayer, on the basis of belief in the unity of God.

In 1830 Ram Mohan Roy came to England on government business, and three years later he died at Bristol, where, be it noted, he was buried with the correct *sraddha*, or Brahmanical burial rites, thus showing that he intended to be thought of as remaining a Hindu to the end. His successors, Keshab Chunder Sen and Pratap Chandra Mozoomdar, were more critical of Western Christianity. Keshab wrote:[6] 'It seems that the Christ who has come to us is an Englishman with English manners and customs about him, and with the temper and spirit of an Englishman in him; why should Hindus go to England to learn Jesus Christ? Is not Christ's native land nearer to India than to England? Are not Jesus and his apostles and immediate followers more akin to Indian nationality than Englishmen?': And Mozoomdar, in his book *The Oriental Christ*, declares:[7] 'When we speak of an Eastern Christ we speak of the incarnation of unbounded love and grace, and when we speak of the Western Christ we speak of the incarnation of theology, formalism, ethical and physical force. Christ, we know, is neither of the East nor of the West, but men have localised what God meant to be universal.'

The sect initiated by Ram Mohan Roy has always remained a small one, and is now believed to be shrinking in numbers—at the last census it was reckoned at about 100,000. Its influence, however, has always been out of proportion to its size. It has had, and still owns, some very distinguished persons among its adherents, and makes a special appeal to educated Indians. Orthodox Hindus naturally regard it as heretical, and it is obviously rather more than a half-way house to liberal Christianity. Yet it is noteworthy that one of the most influential Indian families, that of the Tagores, has from the beginning been a keen supporter of the movement, and has given it generous financial backing. The celebrated Indian poet Rabindranath Tagore (b. 1861) remained a faithful member of it throughout his life, and although this has separated him from the ordinary path of Hinduism, Tagore, next to Gandhi and Nehru, is probably the only distinguished Indian whose

6 India asks Who is Christ?—a lecture given in 1879.
7 *The Oriental Christ*, pp. 43 and 46.

H

name is widely known to the Western world, while in India itself it has become a household word.

Tagore, besides being a poet, a musician, and a dramatist, was also a thinker. He received the Nobel Prize for literature in 1913, and in the same year published his Harvard lectures, entitled *Sadhana* or 'attainment'. In these he made an eloquent appeal for a welding together of the Hindu and Western points of view. He will not praise the mere renunciation of the world as practised by the *sannyasis* or hermits, nor will he commend the bustling activity of the Americans or British, who have, as he says, no interior life at all. He wants mankind to enjoy what is good in both ways of living, 'to belong to God with their souls, and yet to serve Him actively in the world'. Tagore was a faithful nationalist, and whether rightly or wrongly, he claimed this new kind of mysticism as the true ancient wisdom of India. To do this he had to interpret the ancient texts in a rather arbitrary manner, and Schweitzer considers[8] that this was a weakness on his part, since the Vedic texts ought, in strict honesty and in harmony with scientific method, to be taken in the meaning which they originally had. In so far as he picks out life-affirming passages where they occur in the Upanishads, Tagore is justified; but he is not equally justified in slurring over the other passages which have an opposite significance, and which represent the view which was growing and advancing in recognition during the Upanishadic period. To interpret the Upanishads in this way lands one in just as great difficulties as to interpret the Old Testament allegorically. Both methods do violence to history. The truth is that Tagore, in his interpretation of Hindu ideas, shows that through the Brahmo-Samaj and other contacts he has become influenced by Christian theology. Although he remains a Hindu, his Hinduism is strongly tinged with ideas proceeding from another sphere of thought.

The same comments to some degree are valid in respect of two other Hindu philosophers of the modern age, Sri Aurobindo Ghose (b. 1872) and Sri Sarvepalli Radhakrishnan (b. 1888).

Aurobindo Ghose was educated in England, and took a high place in examination. After some time spent in teaching and in political journalism as a nationalist, he retired to Pondicherry in 1910, and adopted the contemplative life, setting up, in correct Hindu fashion, an *ashrama* or school of disciples.

In three large volumes, entitled *The Life Divine*, he has now tried to put forth a synthesis between the ancient Hinduism of the standard sacred books and the modern world of the sciences. He begins by

8 In *Indian Thought and its Development*, pp. 241 ff.

emphasising the two poles which stand in antithesis, the denial of the spiritual by the materialist, and the rejection of the material world by the ascetic. These two negations find their reconciliation, he holds, in the cosmic consciousness. 'Science and Religion are both concerned with the life-process, of which we are luminous self-conscious centres.' Aurobindo then proceeds to interpret his own idea of what is meant by evolution. He sees here an ascending and a descending movement. 'God,'[9] he says, 'descends through an entropy of self-concealment, the main grades being super-mind, higher mind, mind, life, and lastly body or matter. In evolution He recovers Himself by reversing the order, and mounting the steps of the ladder. . . . At every higher step of evolution a power from without enters and descends to the lowest step of the ladder, and then ascends, transforming the nature of every one of the antecedent terms. But this being the case, Mankind is not destined to stop at its present level. It must either fall by the wayside, and leave the victory to other and new creations, or it must aspire to a fresh ascent. . . . Man must either end in death, or else continue as a new being with greater integrity and balance, with a new accession of God within him. . . . And this superman is to be built up by the descent upon humanity of super-mind.'

The reader may think that all this is so much jargon, but it should be remembered that it is the very earnest attempt of a gifted man to make a new synthesis between the scientific standpoint which he has learned during his sojourn in Europe, and the Vedantic monistic religion which he has inherited, and that India is taking him very seriously. There is a striking similarity between Aurobindo's idea of a higher humanity and the Pauline doctrine of a doomed mankind lifted on to a higher level by the second Adam, who is the Lord from Heaven. Aurobindo makes no acknowledgment of any indebtedness to the New Testament, and he does not believe that the New Man has yet come—rather he awaits his coming; but it is difficult not to think that here again we have a Hinduism which is bordering upon some dim apprehension of Christianity. Aurobindo continues throughout his long essay to use the terms and framework of standard Hindu philosophy, such as *Purusha, Ishwara, tāpās,* and *maya,* and his endeavour is in fact to re-write Hinduism, and pave the way for a new system of discipline or *yoga* (q.v.) by which the production of the New Man may be fostered. Each of his chapters has prefixed to it passages from

9 *See* also Mr. P. Chenchiah on *Aurobindo, his Message,* in *The Pilgrim,* vol. iii, July 1943, p. 46.

the Hindu sacred books, and what follows is really an extensive commentary on these texts. In more ways than one he reminds us of some of the famous orientalising Gnostics described by Professor Burkitt in his Donnellan and Mosse Lectures.[10] It is perhaps not an accident that in chapter xxvii of his third volume Aurobindo actually uses the phrase 'the Gnostic being'. It is a *tour de force* for him to have written so long a book in English. Yet his work lacks the disciplined lucidity of a Western thinker such as Bertrand Russell, and the reader becomes wearied by it, and is tempted to wonder whether much of it has any meaning, and even if it has, whether that meaning could not have been more concisely expressed.

Radhakrishnan has spent much of his life in Europe, as a teacher at Oxford. His chief writings are *A History of Indian Philosophy*, *An Idealist View of Life* (Hibbert Lectures 1932), *Eastern Religion and Western Thought*, and a short pamphlet entitled *The Religion We Need*. Briefly he is what may be described as a Hindu modernist. 'The scriptures of an earlier age,'[11] he says, 'cannot answer the problems of our time. The great representatives of Indian culture were men of mobility and ceaseless adventure, and we are not loyal to their spirit if we mark time in a world of perpetual movement, by sitting still and chanting ancient hymns. We cannot command the sun to stand still on the plains of Hindustan. . . .' Such doctrine is hardly likely to be palatable to Hindu traditionalists, and indeed it would seem that Radhakrishnan, with his much greater acquaintance with the West, is moving away from the faith of his fathers, and endeavouring to construct a new synthetic religion which will contain elements borrowed from Europe and Asia alike. It is a valiant attempt, but whether it will satisfy the needs of anyone but the constructor is another question.

Against this, and in contrast with it, is Radhakrishnan's *Hindu View of Life*, in which he tries to conserve and extend what seems to him to be the essence of his ancestral religion. Hinduism as he proclaims it is an attitude rather than a creed. Indians, he would say, have before them the same set of facts of religious experience as other peoples in the world, but it is their approach to these facts which is distinctive. They are tolerant, he declares, and do not persecute. They abhor exclusiveness in religion. They start from the assumption that every people has its contribution to make to the wisdom, understanding, thought, and culture of the human race.

10 *The Religion of the Manichees*, and *Church and Gnosis*.
11 *The Hindu View of Life*, pp. 36–7.

'Hinduism is like a huge reservoir into which each successive race of newcomers has poured its vivifying stream of primitive freshness and vigour. Continuously strengthened and vitalised by these infusions, Hinduism has in its turn enriched the newcomers from its stores of traditional culture. As with peoples, so with their beliefs; Hinduism developed an attitude of comprehensive charity instead of a fanatic faith in an inflexible creed. It accepted the multiplicity of aboriginal gods and others which originated, most of them, outside the Aryan tradition, and justified them all.'

'Hinduism is wholly free from the strange obsession of the Semitic faiths,' he writes (with an eye on Islam quite as much as on Christianity), 'the obsession that the acceptance of a particular religious metaphysic is necessary for salvation, and that non-acceptance thereof is a heinous sin, meriting eternal punishment in hell.'

'Religious beliefs to the Hindu are symbolical . . . our accounts of God are likely stories, but all the same, legendary. . . . We are like little children on the seashore, trying to fill our shells with water from the sea.'[12]

Thus, no religious experience has a final value, though all of it has some, and diversity is to be welcomed, not regretted.

The apologia for Hinduism displayed in these passages is skilful, but an agnostic, quite as much as a Christian or a Moslem, might be tempted to retort that it has about it an air of rationalisation.

For another line of development in reformed or neo-Hinduism we must go back to the year 1875, when Dayanand Sarasvati (1824–1883) founded an association which he called Arya Samaj. Dayanand was a Kathiawar Brahmin, strictly educated in orthodoxy, and the story of his conversion sounds like an echo from the days of the downfall of Sarapis-worship in Egypt. Keeping a vigil as a boy, before the image of Siva, he saw about midnight a mouse leave its hole and run about over the image. From that time he lost his faith in idol-cultus. Shortly after, a young sister of his died, and this brought him abruptly face to face with the ultimate problem of life. He ran away from home to avoid early marriage, and wandered for some years, seeking a spiritual guide. Eventually at Muttra he found a blind teacher, Swami Virjanand, who taught him to discard the later Hinduism, and to return to the study of the Vedas. At the close of his studies he offered the Swami the usual present, but Virjanand would receive none. 'Only,' said he, 'if you would give me anything, let it be this. Impart the knowledge of the ancient religion to the Motherland.' Dayanand did as he was asked, and in the face of considerable opposition began to preach. Finally, he set about organising his society or *sampradaya*, especially

12 Quoted from Professor Joad's *Counter Attack from the East*.

inviting young educated men to join, and in this he met with immediate success.

The new community has since grown to a membership of over half a million, and is still aggressively expanding. Judged from the standpoint of literary criticism, Dayanand's claim for the Vedas cannot be substantiated. The Vedas are not, as he maintained, 'the purest record of the highest form of monotheism that can be conceived'. Nor is it possible truthfully to agree that Copernican astronomy, let alone 'any scientific theory or principle which is thought to be of modern origin', can be proved to be set forth in their pages. Such earnest assertions are only pathetic signs of the inferiority complex from which nineteenth-century Hinduism was suffering. But it is true that in his main contention Dayanand and his *guru* were right. The religion of the Upanishads *is* immeasurably purer and better than the popular Hinduism of the eighteenth and early nineteenth centuries. Moreover, Dayanand's demand that all Hindus, and not only the three highest castes, should have the right to study the sacred books has loosened the bonds of caste and weakened the hold of idolatry, besides diminishing the priestly tyranny of the Brahmins. Dayanand issued his own commentary on the Vedas, called Satyartha Prakash, and this may easily become a new sacred book in his own sect. Arya Samaj has undertaken some praiseworthy unselfish social service among the depressed classes, and possesses good educational institutions. After the death of Swami Dayanand, his movement split into two sections, the one conservative, the other more liberal and advanced. It has now begun to admit outcastes to membership, and is thus undermining the character of the older Hinduism.

Another important reform movement of a similar type began with Gadadhar Chatterji, the son of a poor Bengali Brahmin. From his youth up he showed himself to be a lad of no ordinary quality. He had visions, and eventually retired into the forest, and took the obviously religious name of Ramakrishna Parahamsa. Though a thoroughgoing Hindu, trained in meditation and in the study of the Upanishads, he continued his wanderings, and learnt much from contact with a Moslem *sufi* or mystic, and also from a Christian missionary. Finally he settled down at (of all places!) the temple of Kali near Calcutta, and there held converse with any Hindu seekers who came to him. Among these was Keshab Chunder Sen, who, in his day, as we have seen, was responsible for some of the earlier developments of the Brahmo-Samaj. But Ramakrishna's most famous pupil was a brilliant young Bengali of high caste, Narendranath Datta (1862–1902), better known by his later name of Swami Vivekananda. Vivekananda was a typical westernised Indian, who had received a thorough modern education. After studying mid-nineteenth-century rationalism, he found that it gave him no lasting satisfaction, and finally, in 1884, after the loss of his estate, he came, through despair and anguish, to seek peace in the company of Ramakrishna. The simple and earnest piety of the latter deeply moved him, and after the death of his teacher Vivekananda devoted the remainder of his life to the proclamation of what he believed to be the world message of Ramakrishna. The latter had been of no great intellectual eminence, but he was undoubtedly a singularly effective advocate of devotion or *bhakti*, which each man, he said, should endeavour to practise within his own sect or denomination. 'Every religion becomes true, when he who believes in it dedicates himself to the love of God and the service of his fellow-men.'

Although Vivekananda set himself to propagate this, he showed himself on one side strongly conservative. Thus, while he proclaimed an esoteric teaching for an inner circle, he gave permission for the vast majority of Hindus to go on with their old ritual and mythology, and like Plutarch, he allegorised the coarseness of the myths to explain it away, and so to make them intelligible and tolerable for the educated. But Vivekananda did much more than this. The identity of the self with Brahman according to him was to be achieved not only by the usual contemplative exercises, but also by absorption in active selfless service. Following up this line, he inaugurated the Ramakrishna Mission, which has ever since performed fine work among the poor and sick of India. Vivekananda was, in his own way, a student of the New Testament, and though he displayed in the course of his life some very human weaknesses, and not a little vanity, he did, in the opinion of C. F. Andrews, 'a very great work indeed in leavening the more reactionary Hinduism with new and liberal ideas'.

Another and in many ways far more attractive character was a neo-Vedantist of North India, Swami Ram Tirath, a professor of mathematics who gave up his college work to become a wandering ascetic teacher, living alone in the wild parts of the Himalayas. Though he was a genuine Hindu, there is a much stronger and deeper Christian note in Ram Tirath's writings than in those of Vivekananda. He was drowned in the Punjab just as his genius seemed to be nearing fruition.

The last Hindu reformer to be considered here is Justice Ranade of Bombay. Ranade is in many ways the best and wisest of his group. He was the first indigenous Fellow of Bombay University to be appointed, and after a distinguished academic career, he rose in his profession to

the position of Judge of the High Court. In his directly religious work
he was a founder of the Prarthana Samaj or Prayer Society, a similar
body to the Brahmo-Samaj, but with a great interest in social service.
Ranade's attitude towards Hinduism can best be indicated by two
quotations from his writings which show the soundness and clarity
of his thought, as well as his extremely forward-looking view of his
own religion.

(1) 'We represent in India a continuity of creed, traditions, literature,
philosophy, modes of life, and forms of thought which are peculiar to this
land. It cannot surely be for nothing that this peculiar favour has been
shown to us under providential guidance. If the miraculous preservation
of a few thousand Jews had a purpose, this more miraculous preservation
of one-fifth of the human race is not due to mere chance. We are under the
severe discipline of a high purpose. . . . Change for the better by slow and
gradual absorption and assimilation, not by sudden conversion and revolution—this has been the characteristic feature of our past history.'

(2) 'With too many of us a thing is true or false, right or sinful, simply
because some one in the past has said so. The new idea which must take
place of this helplessness and dependence is not the idea of rebellious over-
throw of all authority, but that of freedom responsible to the voice of
God in us. . . . The new idea that should come in is that the law of *karma*[13]
can be controlled and set back by a properly trained will made subservient to
a Higher Will than ours—the Will of God. With regard to the old idea
that human life is a vanity, a dream, and that we are not much concerned
with it—a healthy sense of the true dignity of our nature and of man's high
destiny is the best corrective and antidote to this poison.'

*   *   *   *   *

Perhaps it ought to be said that one of the chief social reforms which
is desired by these earnest men is the abolition of caste distinctions. It
must not be supposed that efforts to abolish caste and idolatry have
always succeeded in recent years. These institutions have often returned
again just where they seemed to have been given up. But it is most
significant that Hindus of influence, from Tagore to Nehru and from
Gandhi to Ranade, have all united in saying that the regeneration of
Indian life depends directly and perhaps solely upon the removal of
the condition of caste, and curiously enough, any rumour of the
slightest weakening or concession among Christians in this direction
has called forth a stream of indignation from the Hindu-controlled
newspapers.

13 *See* chapter 3, p. 52.

We may sum up at the end of this chapter by saying that the real point for which Hindus seem to stand at present is for their right to reform and re-shape their own religion themselves, and they apparently have confidence that they are able to do it. Their success or failure can only be left to the judgment of time.

BOOKS FOR FURTHER STUDY

The Cambridge History of India. Vol. vi.

The Shorter Cambridge History of India.

ABBÉ JEAN ANTOINE DUBOIS, ed. Beauchamp. Oxford. 1906.

M. MONIER WILLIAMS. *Hinduism*.

SWAMI VIVEKANANDA. *opera*.

RABINDRANATH TAGORE. *opera*.

C. F. ANDREWS. *North India* (S.P.G. Manuals). *The Renaissance in India*.

PROFESSOR RADHAKAMAL MUKERJEE. *The Theory and Art of Mysticism*.

PROFESSOR SARVEPALLI RADHAKRISHNAN. *opera*, and especially *The Hindu View of Life*.

SRI AUROBINDO GHOSE. *The Divine Life*. Madras. 1938.

PANDIT NEHRU. op. cit. last four chapters.

9

RELIGIOUS OBSERVANCES

HINDUISM AS A WORKING SYSTEM

The reader who has followed the argument of the book up to this point
will probably feel that in spite of the evidence about reforming movements which was given in the last chapter, he would like to know how
Hinduism works in the daily life of the average believer.

To give this in any detail would involve more space than is here
available. It took, for instance, a whole book of 474 pages for Mrs.
Sinclair Stevenson to recount the ordinary rites which the high-caste
observant Hindu has to perform during his lifetime. But a few general
remarks can usefully be made, and I will group them under eight
headings.

I. TYPES:

Dr. Somervell, medical officer to some of the Mount Everest expeditions, who has spent many years in South India as a doctor, and
knows the people well, has given it as his opinion that there are two
clear types of Hinduism, the spiritual and the popular, and that between
them there is an enormous gap, far greater than that which exists
between popular and philosophical Christianity. Indians themselves
would, however, distinguish three types, to which we have already
referred, *jñānayoga*, *bhaktiyoga*, and *karmayoga*. Although the first two
might be called spiritual, there is a profound difference between the
religion of the philosopher and that of the emotional theist. Somervell
goes on to describe how he saw a large bevy of peasants performing
puja in front of an enormous ant-heap, because some credulous person
had declared that supernatural sounds had been heard coming out of

it, and he adds that an educated Hindu standing by had said to him, 'Even this somewhat naïve and degraded worship is the adoration of the Supreme Deity Who is worshipped by you Christians.' It is inconceivable that the peasants thought of what they were doing in this way, and so long as illiteracy is widespread, it is unlikely that any sophisticated explanation would occur to them. Indeed, elementary education would probably lead to a speedy cessation of such practices. Many critics will assert that statements like that of the educated bystander would hardly be made if it were not for the anxiety of the nationalist to justify his own countrymen in the eyes of observers. But this does not seem quite fair, since for some centuries similar explanations have been current in India. A French traveller, Bernier, heard one at Benares as far back as 1665. It is just possible that they were called forth, in defence, by the entry of Moslem propaganda into the country.

2. POLYTHEISM:

An American once described the Japanese picturesquely as 'an A.D. people with a B.C. mind'. This might very well be applied to considerable numbers of Hindus. Although a certain proportion of them are monotheists, or even philosophers who practise an inward worship of the Impersonal, a large percentage are still believers in gods many and lords many. These latter have their own specially Indian local characteristics, but a polytheist of ancient Greece or Rome would understand them well enough. Thus Brahma, who in the Vedas is 'Lord of Creation', is still to many, like Zeus, 'Father of gods and men'; Krishna is the Indian Apollo, Kamadeva the Indian Eros. Other deities are more difficult to parallel. Siva has been compared since the days of Megasthenes to Dionysus, whom he resembles to the extent of being both orgiastic and dangerous. But there is no necessary generic connexion between the two gods. Similarly Sarasvati, the goddess of learning, bears some resemblance to Pallas Athene, but again there is no connexion. Then there are the various *avatars* of Vishnu (other than Krishna), to whom Jagannath is a late and purely mythical but very popular addition, coming into the Hindu pantheon much as Mithras did into that of late Graeco-Roman antiquity. And then further, there are all kinds of minor deities, connected it may be with heavenly bodies, or with local objects of importance such as trees and stones, deified heroes, some of them even British; and a number of sacred rivers, especially the Ganges and the Nerbudda, and five holy lakes. The malevolent numinous is represented by the goddess of smallpox (called Sitala in North India and Mariamma in the South), and of cholera, which is sometimes connected with Kali, sometimes with Mari Mai, who is said to be the sister of Sitala. Then there is snake-worship, especially that of Manasa, who is called the Queen of the snakes, and is invoked to protect people against snakebite. There is also the cult of half-animal deities such as Ganesa of the elephant head, the god of wisdom and learning, partly a quasi-totemistic creature, partly perhaps a half-forgotten memory of some aboriginal beings called 'monkeys' by the proto-Nordic invaders. These two latter obviously resemble some of the half-animal gods of ancient Egypt, and may merely signify the worship of the Power of Life in its sub-human forms, especially if associated with animal cunning and crafty intelligence.

How much of this pluralism is likely to survive the spread of literacy is uncertain. Already one hears of ceremonial observances being given up by the younger generation, and there are, as we have already recorded (and shall record again), positive attempts on the part of intelligent Hindus at unifying this jungle of divinities, by saying that each is only a symbol of some aspect of the Spirit of Life; and this mode of thought as we have seen is very ancient.[1]

3. DHARMA:

This important word stands for many things, and in its Pali form *dhamma*, it occurs as a basic term in Buddhism. In popular Hinduism it means one's ideal duty, the right behaviour according to the station in life in which one has been placed by Providence. Thus its immediate application lies in the performance of the duties appropriate to one's caste, which may be ceremonial rather than moral, and may involve merely keeping such taboos as not eating, drinking, or smoking with other castes, not eating prohibited food, and not engaging in a for-bidden occupation. The standard of purity is largely artificial. Breaches of this *dharma* are punishable by a caste council, which can inflict penances, such as the taking of what has been called 'the penitential pill', made out of the five products of the cow, and sometimes a pilgrimage. Small fines may be imposed for petty offences, and for the gravest there may be excommunication. Some of the ordinary criminal acts, such as adultery, seduction, and assault, may also be dealt with, but it does not follow that the penalties imposed for these will be as severe as in a civil code, and since the actual powers of the caste councils may vary very much from caste to caste—while different castes have even different views as to what constitutes immoral behaviour—the value of caste discipline may easily be exaggerated. If there is a difference on a

1 *See* p. 45-6.

specific point between the caste view of morality and that of the general moral consciousness of mankind, there is a likelihood that the caste view will be preferred.

Dharma under some circumstances simply means religion, under others it means righteousness or justice, and sometimes it seems to be an abstract equivalent of 'God', not unlike such a phrase as 'The Divine Imperative'.

When it is said that the whole life of a Hindu is regulated by religion, even the cooking of his food, it is largely a ritual regulation that is meant, and this is to some degree similar to the ritual regulation in the Torah which controls the life of a conservative and orthodox Jew, and the arguments by which it is justified are very similar in each case. The ceremonial *dharma* and the food and washing regulations of the Torah alike are recognised as a discipline of the body, and they are not enjoined upon persons who are not Hindus or Jews.

But *dharma* may be used also to signify something much nobler. It has been described as the primary purpose of life, namely to move in harmony with the great vital Force which sustains the universe in its entirety, such things as speaking the truth, forgiveness, self-control, study or research, patience, and the spiritual quest.

It is said that the Vedas prescribe four chief ends in life. First, the observance of *dharma*. Secondly, the earning of one's living. Third, the enjoyment of the legitimate pleasures of life. Fourth, the re-absorption of the individual life into that of the Great Self.

In South India a number of moral treatises have been in circulation for many centuries, mostly written in the Tamil tongue. Of these, by far the most important are the Kurral and the Naladiyar. The former, which is possibly second-century A.D., consists of 400 quatrains. Being in verse, they are easy to memorise, and their ethical level is very high, and often approximates to that of Christianity. The Kurral is curious, in that it hardly mentions Deity, and shows no concern with Brahmanic philosophy or ritual, while it sets the householder's life above that of the ascetic. One wonders in what circles it originated.[2] The young learn such moral precepts along with their alphabet in the village schools, and although there is no doctrine of sin or grace which accompanies the proverbs, they have much the same effect upon the training of the character as the 'two duties' in the Anglican Prayer Book Catechism.

2 Bishop Neill considers that the Kurral is probably third-century A.D., though it may lie anywhere between the second and the fifth centuries, and that its curiously non-theistic character is due to Jain influence.

In the main, there is practically no systematic religious teaching in these schools, and except whatever may be given by the *gurus* (who are the nearest equivalent that Hinduism possesses to the pastoral ministers of Christendom) such teaching has to be imparted by the parents themselves. This, in principle, is not a bad thing. The *gurus* as a class are on the whole virtuous and earnest men, but they only pay occasional and intermittent visits to the families in their charge. The impartiality of the British Raj has led to the exclusion of religious teaching from the state-aided schools of India, and this has had the same effect as in other countries of producing a generation divorced from its traditional faith.

4. WORSHIP:

It must be said, first of all, that except where *bhakti* devotees assemble for a *kirtan*, or *bhajan* (hymn-singing), there is no such thing as congregational worship in the sense in which it is known by Christians. Hindu worship is of two kinds; (*a*) domestic; (*b*) temple, but (*a*) is private, and (*b*) is performed either by priests, with individuals merely acting as spectators, or by individuals who go through some private act of *puja* or devotion.

(*a*) *Domestic worship*. The ordinary Hindu dwelling may have a sort of prayer-room or private chapel in it, containing appropriate religious images or sacred symbols. These may consist of actual idols, which have gone through a process of *pranpratishta*, 'quickening', or 'consecration', so that they are not merely symbols, but effectual localised means of contact with Deity—quite as effectual, in fact, to those who faithfully use them as the Host in the Tabernacle of a Catholic church. Such objects may or may not be anthropomorphic, and among Vaishnavites the favourite ones may be either a *tulasi* or basil plant in a pot (which is regarded as a sacrament of the presence of Vishnu, and which is lovingly tended by the wife of the household) or else a *salagrama* stone, which is a species of fossil ammonite. In a Saivite household the *lingam* will be the focus of devotion. It is an unkind error to think that this is still regarded by worshippers as a phallus, though it certainly was such in origin. It is now completely detached from all sexual connexions for (one may say) 99 per cent of the worshippers, and I have even heard it described as representing 'the rod of continence'. This means, of course, that its symbolism has been sublimated, since the myth which explains why it is specifically the symbol of Siva leaves no doubt as to its genesis. Where a god is represented in human form, there will actually be ceremonies of waking up, washing, dressing, offering food, putting to rest, and so on. At home women often adore a small brass image of the infant Krishna. Flowers may be offered, or lighted lamps waved ceremoniously in front of it. Sometimes the same kind of honours are paid to the *lingam* as though it were an anthropomorphic image. The name of the god may be called upon with frequency, and short prayers and sacred sentences or *mantras*, such as the *gayatri*, may be recited. This *mantra* is as much a favourite as the Lord's Prayer with Christians, and is regarded with the utmost reverence. Just as the Lord's Prayer was by early Christians said in secret, so the *gayatri* is not supposed to be heard by non-Hindus. One learned Hindu who allowed me to be present while he recited it said it was actually making a concession and granting me a great privilege—and I felt that he certainly was, and appreciated his courtesy. The *gayatri* has been translated in various ways, but the most commonly acceptable English version runs: 'Let us meditate on the most excellent light of the Creator; may He guide our intellects.' This verse is not only repeated to boys at their investiture with the sacred thread, but is used as grace at meals, and as a benediction over the food. It is said that every householder and every Brahmin is expected during his lifetime to recite it 2,400,000 times. The rosary is often employed to check the number of recitations. Mrs. Sinclair Stevenson records that a wealthy Hindu who is uncertain in his later years whether he has performed this duty can make up for lost time by paying a number of Brahmins to perform a service of repetition, which involves not only saying the *gayatri*, but also performing the *homa* sacrifice 240,000 times. The average cost of such a ritual is estimated at about 2,000 rupees.

Passages from the sacred books such as the *Ramayana* or the *Gita* may also be read or meditated upon. O'Malley says that elderly women spend much of their time during the day reading in this manner.

Whether a priest or *purohit* is employed in the home will depend very much upon the income of the individual householder. In a Brahmin house the observant Brahmin should rise two hours before sunrise, and should spend a good deal of his day offering sacrifice with the correct ritual, or engaging in a kind of office. This latter is called the *sāndhya*, and it should be gone through three times during the day, at the beginning, at midday, and in the evening. Brahmins engaged in business will generally perform *sāndhya* twice, either morning and evening, or midday and evening. The office includes the recitation of the *gayatri*, and its central feature is the *pranayama* or breathing exercise, which should be gone through three times in each *sāndhya*, accompanied by the saying of the *gayatri*. Acts of expiation for sins committed are also part of the daily *sāndhya*, and certain ceremonies connected with the freeing of the sun from dangerous influences. Besides the *sāndhya* the Brahmin has twice a day to offer the *homa* sacrifice. This is an offering made to the god of fire, and it is obviously an ancient rite dating from the Vedic period. The small domestic altar used is made of copper, broad at the top and narrow at the base. The altar fire is in ordinary cases brought from the common hearth, and the connexion between the rite and the larger one of the *agnihotra* mentioned in the Upanishads will be evident. The officiant begins by sipping water, and performing *pranayama*. Next he says a kind of invocation, asking the god to come and take up his abode in the altar fire. Then he stands up, takes three blades of grass and puts them into the altar fire, announcing that the oblation is ready, and asking the god to receive it. The actual oblation is then made. First water is poured round the altar, and then two separate offering are made, consisting of *ghee* or clarified butter, rice, rice pudding, or milk. The oblation has to be completely covered with embers. At the same time, in the morning *homa*, two oblations are made, one to the sun and one to Prajapati, the Creator. After a prayer to the sun, the officiant marks his forehead with some of the ashes from the altar, and bowing to the latter requests the god to depart.

Another duty of the devout Brahmin is to read the scriptures every day. This is called *brahmayajna* or alternatively *svadhyaya*. Most of the Brahmins who were consulted by Mrs. Sinclair Stevenson said that they planned to repeat or read through some religious classic every year, so that by the end of their lives they should have read through at least the four Vedas, the great commentaries, the two great epics, and the famous grammar by Panini. The end of the year for these lections to be finished is in mid-August, when the sacred thread is changed. Other ceremonies during a Brahmin's day are offerings to the ancestors, and to the individual's special tutelary deities.

Besides the *purohit*, other types of sacred men are esteemed, the *guru* or spiritual teacher, the *sadhu* or *sannyasi*, both of them wandering or detached ascetics, and the *bhagat*, or emotional devotee, who remains within the social structure of the village, and who is said to be greatly revered by villagers as an exorcist.

(*b*) *Temple worship*. Temples are very numerous in South India, but not so numerous in the North. Mr. P. V. Jagadisa Ayyar has made an illustrated record of over two hundred, some of them very elaborate and magnificent, with immense repetitive ornament. In lay-out and cumulative effect some of these bear an uncanny resemblance to the reconstructed picture of the great abbey at Bury St. Edmunds, with its boundary walls and gates, and an immense central sanctuary surrounded by ancillary and daughter-churches. Very probably the layout at Glastonbury would have looked much the same when it was all in being. Northern temples are chiefly distinguished by having ribbed spires or *sikhara*; Southern by their pyramidal gateways or *gopuras*. The most prolific period of temple-building seems to run parallel with the medieval period in Europe, but some temples are as late as the sixteenth and eighteenth centuries, and as we saw in the introduction, fine modern ones are still being built. Probably in most areas the men do not go to the temple more than once or twice a year, though they maintain their Brahmins with food, venerate their local godlings, and once annually go with their women to make offerings at the yearly festival of the local shrine, very much as an English villager will go to church at Easter or at Harvest Thanksgiving. These local temples are, of course, only modest affairs, and stand to the big ones more in the ratio of a small mission church to a great cathedral. Mr. Natarajan, the Brahmo Samaj editor of the *Indian Social Reformer*, says that the temples are being attended to a diminishing extent, and even pictures the time when they will be preserved as ancient monuments. But, of course, there may be some sort of revival, and in any case the practice varies from district to district just as church-attendance does in Europe. Photographs of the new Lakshmi-Narayan temple at Delhi show that it attracts very large crowds. The temple is essentially the house of the god conceived as a celestial raja. Hence the ceremonies of waking, washing, feeding and entertaining which we noticed in regard to the domestic shrine are performed here on a much larger and more elaborate scale. Hence also the presence of huge offerings of food, and the maintenance of establishments of dancing girls, as well as of temple prostitutes, or *devadasis*, since it is assumed that the god requires wives. The central court with its great image is where the god gives audience. To the sophisticated mystic all this paraphernalia seems useless, but although such persons are even actually to be found within the temple precincts, they are quite tolerant towards what goes on around them, and say that it is *karma-marga* or the way of works, permissible for those who feel the need of it, and who have not reached to the higher stages of the spiritual life.

5. LIFE:

The division of life into four stages or *ashramas* is still recognised,

I

that of the student, the householder, the hermit, and the ascetic. Before they begin, the boy is regarded as an infant.

The famous investiture with the sacred thread usually takes place at the age of eight, though under certain circumstances it may be postponed until the age of sixteen, and it may take place in the eleventh year with a member of a warrior group and in the twelfth with a Vaisya. The ceremony is a very long and complicated one, and cannot be told here in detail, but the central features are those of a puberty initiation, with great elaboration throughout, and the whole rite takes more than three days to complete. It is in some ways a pity that many of the disciplinary features of the life of the fully initiated lad are today in process of disintegration. Rules of study, avoidance of luxury, and endurance of hardship are only too often disregarded, and with this break-up of the old Brahmin piety much good is being lost.

6. FESTIVALS:

Reference has already been made to the Festival of Light or Dewali. Nothing is more certain than the value of the succession of festivals in making and preserving popular Hinduism as a living religion to the masses. The precise number of such great days of observance varies in different localities. Thus the Bengal government declared twenty-three days and the Punjab government ten as public holidays on account of these ceremonial gatherings. Mrs. Stevenson gives an account of the entire sacred year of the Brahmins, month by month, and the details remind one of those given in the Fasti of Ovid with regard to the Roman calendar. One of the most extraordinary of these festivals is Holi, which occurs in the February or March period, and lasts three days. It is accompanied by the burning of a great bonfire, and indulgence in much ceremonial obscenity. More thoughtful Hindus are inclined to advocate the abolition or at least the restriction or reform of the Holi ceremonies, which are obviously a survival of magical fertility rites from earlier ages of the world, and in their present degraded form are at worst very evil or at least very foolish. Another curious festival is the day of Ayudah puja, when every craftsman worships the tools of his or her craft, whether they be pens, paper, farm implements, or machinery. Animal sacrifice of a calf, or a sheep or goat, has been known to be made to the machines in a cotton mill, or even to a motor-bicycle. Then there is the festival held in the month of Sravana in honour of the goddess of smallpox. Mrs. Stevenson gives a vivid and sympathetic account of this:

'Of all *melas* (festivals) this is the one that the writer loves best to watch. Down below at the riverside is a regular fair, with merry-go-rounds, and glittering stalls of mirrors, toys, and fruit; up the narrow lane that climbs to the shrine throng pleasant family groups of mothers and children, clad in their brightest blues and greens and reds. Arrived at the shrine, the happy mothers whose children have been guarded all the year from every childish ailment, chicken-pox, scarlet fever, German measles, as well as from small-pox, deposit in front of the goddess coconuts or handfuls of flowers, salt, or grain, and little pots of whey, oil, treacle, or clarified butter. Some even go so far as to offer a tiny model of an umbrella, the sign of royalty or divinity (for every god loves an umbrella); or a silver eye, when delivered from ophthalmia. Or you might see a child being weighed against sugar or dates, in fulfilment of a vow made during illness. It adds to the fun, that the officiant at the shrine only keeps half the offerings for himself and distributes the rest amongst the children present. Within the enclosure round the shrine there is practically not a man to be seen, only the happy women with their sweet faces (for this is a festival which attracts the nicest type of women, especially Brahman and Kanabi), rejoicing in true mother-fashion at the restoration of their sick children to health or praying for their preservation during the coming year. In the sunshine the charming scene glows like a veritable tulip-garden and all seems fragrant with mother-love.'[3]

7. VOWS AND PILGRIMAGES:

The vow, which is universal in human religious devotion, is an important item in connexion with Indian temples and shrines. It takes many forms, sometimes the bestowal of presents, perhaps the weight of the person concerned in some form of food or valuables, the digging of wells, the founding of a sacred institution, or the writing of the name of the god hundreds of thousands of times: but the object is always either to procure some benefit or favour or to make expiation for some supposed transgression. Circumambulation of a sacred object, whether a *tulasi* plant, a tree, or a building, is one form of carrying out a vow. Others may be eating without the use of one's hands, going without salt, or even mutilating the body with skewers. (Many of these are also customs among Moslem devotees, and self-flagellation as a votive act is, of course, recognised among Catholic Christians as part of the filling up of the measure of the sufferings of Christ.) Everyone will admit the obligation to undertake at some time or other the performance of a pilgrimage, and vast crowds gather, for example, to bathe in the sacred waters of the Ganges at Allahabad. It was one of these gatherings that Aldous Huxley had in mind when he made a character in one of his novels, seeing the spectacle, murmur

3 Mrs. Sinclair Stevenson. *The Rites of the Twice Born*, pp. 306–7.

gently: 'If I were an Indian millionaire, I should feel like spending some of my fortune in the endowment of atheist propaganda.' Yet there are pilgrimages of varying degrees and quality, and he would indeed be unsympathetic who did not concede that some of these bring very real happiness and a sense of liberation to those who take part in them. O'Malley records that in 1932 a special pilgrim train, in which passengers lived and slept, went all over India, visiting dozens of sacred centres in the minimum of time and with the minimum of trouble and fatigue to the devotees, while an airstrip has been constructed at an altitude of 10,000 feet in the Himalayas to enable pilgrims to travel by air to the shrine of Badrinath in Garhwal. Applied science is thus making the acquisition of merit much easier than heretofore. But some pilgrimages are still difficult. One Saivite place of pilgrimage, the cave of Amarnath in Kashmir, is such a dangerous journey that a few years ago, out of a total of 12,000 pilgrims, 500 died on the way.

8. YOGA:

Of all countries in the world India still contains the largest number of persons leading, or at any rate professing to lead, lives of asceticism. Their principles may be gathered from the names by which they are known: *sadhu*, 'holy man'; *sannyasi*, 'one who abandons the world' (Saivite); *bairagi*, the same term for a Vaisnavite; *gosain*, 'one who is lord of his passions'; *yogi*, 'one who seeks union with Deity'; *bhagat*, 'saint' or 'blessed one'. *Fakir*, or 'mendicant', is a Moslem not a Hindu term, and should not be applied to non-Moslems.

We have already seen something of the doctrinal basis for this retirement from the world. The aim is the mystical identification with the Supreme Absolute Being by giving up all worldly ties, and eradicating all desire and all passion. The body is to be cleansed and disciplined by a prescribed technique, and the mind brought strictly under control. This may involve the entrance of the individual upon the third and fourth *ashramas* as permanent states of life, or it may mean a temporary retreat, having its counterpart in the periodic retirement of the Catholic Christian for the purpose of 'making his soul'—which is the recognised expression. Or again it may mean the embracing of a special vocation to an ascetic life at a relatively early age, a step which also has its counterpart in Christianity. It is startling to Westerners to find that an apparently prosperous Hindu business man will, in his later years, often leave his home and family, wind up his affairs, and retire permanently to a life of meditation. Certain temperaments in almost any part of the world may elect to do this. We may recall how George Fox records that at a crisis in his life from which he never looked back he 'broke off all familiarity with old and young'. But even Hindus who are still concerned with their professions will from time to time disappear in order to engage in a protracted retreat under the guidance of some expert ascetic. Thus a distinguished medical specialist with a full European training some years ago posted a notice on the door of his laboratory to the effect that he was intending to be absent for several weeks for such a purpose, and his departure was taken completely for granted by his colleagues, and excited no more comment than would that of an Englishman who had announced that he would be absent from his clinic in order to attend a scientific congress.

The actual total number of ascetics of a permanent sort in India is difficult to compute, for the reasons given above. Thus as many as fifty or sixty thousand have been known to attend the great bathing festival of the Kumba Mela at Allahabad, but how many of these were, so to speak, professional life-long ascetics, how many persons in the third and fourth *ashramas* and how many mere temporary *sadhus*, it is not easy to ascertain.[4] Perhaps the Indian census returns may give us some indication, and in these it would appear that recently about one in eighty of the population registered as following the vocation of a professional ascetic. The numbers are known to have diminished in the last fifty years, and the percentage may still be decreasing.

As we know to have been the case in medieval Europe, so now in India today, some of these holy persons on closer contact prove to be anything but holy, but the impartial testimony of experienced observers tends to show that very many, possibly the majority, whether unattached or as members of a *math* or order, are quiet, peaceable folk, exercising a wholesome influence upon the people in their neighbourhood. Sir Denzil Ibbetson wrote of such in the Punjab: 'There is an immense number of these men whose influence is wholly for good': and Sir Bamfylde Fuller, writing of similar persons in Assam: 'They inculcate in their disciples pure morality; their influence is altogether for good.' It must, however, be admitted that a morbid preoccupation with religion has reduced a good many to the level of pathological specimens, to wit the type described by Dr. John Wilson of the Free

4 Professor Hutton thinks that census figures are likely to give an unduly low estimate, as probably many *sadhus* do not get registered. On the other hand he considers that an appreciable number of quasi-ascetics are fugitives from justice or escaped criminals. The *sadhu's* livery of ashes is a very convenient form of disguise, and indeed affords a kind of travelling sanctuary.

Church of Scotland, 'whose nails were grown into his cheeks, and who had a bird's nest upon his head', and who in answer to an inquiry, replied: 'Do not ask me questions. You may look at me, for I am Brahman.' Such a person would in Europe be regarded as certifiable.

Although *yogis* may belong to any sect or to none, a majority may be Saivites, since Siva is reputed to be the supreme ascetic, and the inventor of *yoga*.

The word *yoga* is now well known both in Europe and America, but its meaning is much misunderstood by the public, who think that it means little more than sitting in curious postures. This is a complete mistake. The physical side is only the preparatory stage, and is devised in order to secure poise, bodily fitness, and calm self-control. In this it is undoubtedly successful. The divisions of the subject are variously conceived. A good number of authorities recognise only two grades, *hatha yoga*, or the physical training, and *raja yoga*, or the mental training. But there is also a fuller analysis into:

1. *Krija yoga*, or preparatory exercises;
2. *Bhakti yoga*, or union by love;
3. *Karma yoga*, or union by works;
4. *Jñana yoga*, or union by knowledge;
5. *Hatha yoga*, or union by physical exercises;
6. *Raja yoga*, or union by will.

This latter analysis implies a broader definition of what *yoga* actually is and may be. Indeed, it almost makes it identical with religious activity of every kind. Still, for most people the last two divisions correspond with what is usually implied in the words 'contemplative union with Absolute Deity'. There are, of course, other divisions, such as *mantra yoga*, or the repetition of a sacred sentence, and *laya yoga* or concentration.

As a rule, whoever seeks to practise *yoga* will select a spiritual director or *guru*. This custom has its parallel in Catholicism (*see* Pascal, Fr. Poulain, and Dom Bede Frost). A woman, it is said, may act as *guru* to her son. *Gurus* are often treated by their disciples with divine honours. The goal sought after is called *samadhi*, or a specially exalted state of consciousness, which may be of two kinds:

(*a*) *samprajnata samadhi*, or *samadhi* with discrimination of one's own separate personality;
(*b*) *asamprajnata samadhi*, or *samadhi* without discrimination of one's own separate personality.

The preliminary training, or *hatha yoga*, consists in breathing-control, in ablutions, internal and external, and in the practice of a number of *asanas* or bodily postures. There is, or at any rate need be, nothing specifically religious about these (except for one who believes that the body is the Temple of the Holy Ghost), and any doctor might well prescribe them as a course of treatment for a nerve-patient. They are the direct opposite of violent exercise and 'physical jerks'. India has known pastimes of the latter description, but the *asana* method is perhaps her own special contribution to mental and bodily hygiene. Thus Mr. James Laver has written: 'Far too many people in the West think that they are somehow lowering the status of the mind if they admit that it can be influenced by trifling bodily adjustments. The Hindu thinkers are wiser. They have reared a whole system on these psycho-physical correspondences which to them seem so obvious as to need no discussion. And most of all they realise how important it is not to go about with every nerve in a tight little knot. . . . You will not make the taxi go any faster by screwing up your body and hanging on to the seat with whitened knuckles. You will not make the train come in sooner by stamping up and down, twitching your fingers and your facial muscles, knitting your brows and biting your lips.' One *guru* said to Miss Tillyard: 'You get into your *asana* as a tired man gets into his hot bath'. She adds that many *yogis* seem to attain to an extraordinary control over their bodies, such, for example, as the regulation of the heart-beats, and of the action of the internal organs.

The next stage is what may be called ethical preparation, and includes the practice of *ahimsa*, continence, truthfulness, etc.

Raja yoga is made up of a considerable number of exercises in mental self-control, leading through complete mastery of the will to concentration upon the Absolute. It is, perhaps, describable as a technique for overcoming wandering thoughts, since anyone who has tried to practise the realisation of the Presence of God is only too painfully aware how hard it is to keep the attention centred for any length of time upon the Self-Existent. *Raja yoga*, therefore, begins with quite elementary practice in concentration upon some small object such as a red flower, or a geometrical figure like a yellow square or a blue circle. The significance of the symbol (square = earth or water, circle = air) rather than the symbol itself should be the object of meditation, and *pratyahara*, or the banishment of intruding thoughts, should be firmly practised. Anyone who has read a Catholic treatise on mental prayer will probably wonder how much of this technique has penetrated into Christian practice through the oriental monasteries of (say) East Syria, or whether it may not have come through Neo-Platonism, since something of the kind seems to have been known to Plotinus. It is, of course, also possible that Greeks in the time of Seleucus introduced it into the West after their stay in the Punjab.

Another prescribed exercise is listening to the sounds in one's own ears, which, in an advanced stage of concentration, may signify the *Sabha* or internal voice of the Supreme Life-Force. It does not seem to have occurred to the enthusiasts for this episode in yogic practice that what may have been needed was merely a little aural irrigation. Then there may be meditation upon one's dreams, or upon the various symbolic forms of Deity. The latter meditation is said to lead to the ultimate conclusion that all religions are merely aspects of one truth. Hence there should be no persecution, since truth is one. It is, however, quite possible to arrive at an agreement that persecution is evil without necessarily accepting the argument from *yoga*, which is based solely upon introspection, without any empirical study of external data. Or again, one may meditate upon the life of some Hindu saint, or upon a text from the Vedas. Less edifying topics for meditation are the tip of the nose, 'in order to experience the Absolute Smell', or the elephant, 'in order to acquire strength'.

The progress of the *yogi*, according to one authority, is sevenfold:

(a) longing after truth, or *subchechcha*, which in Christian phraseology would mean 'practice of a detached habit of mind'.

(b) right inquiry, or *vicharana*. This would correspond to discursive meditation.

(c) the fading out of the mind, or *tanamasana*. This would be the prayer of simplicity, or the prayer of quiet.

(d) attainment to conscious unity, or *satvapatti*. This is a realisation of the Upanishadic principle, *tat tvam asi*, thou art That, i.e., the Absolute Being. As far as this point the *samadhi* is said to be *samprajnata*, or *savikalpa*, with consciousness of the finite ego as well as of the Great Self still persisting. In the stages which follow duality is surpassed, and the *samadhi* is said to become *asamprajnata*. These stages are:

(e) indifference to externals, or *asamsakta*.

(f) sensation that things external to Brahma do not exist, or *padarthanabhavana*.

(g) continuous ecstasy, or perpetual *samadhi*.

It is said that only the seventh or last stage cannot be paralleled in Christian mysticism, but this must mean that some mystics, such as

Eckhart, bordered dangerously upon a pantheism which is excluded by the genuine Catholic doctrine of Divine Transcendence. Actually it is a question of what Eckhart really meant when he spoke of the soul being swallowed up in Deity, since he balances it at other times by statements which sound perfectly orthodox, but may, of course, be interpolations in his work.

The problem which the impartial spectator feels bound to consider is whether the state of perpetual *samadhi* is compatible with world-transforming activity, or even with any measure of social service at all. This is precisely the point at which the Indian reformers have stepped in as we noted in the preceding chapter. But the same problems exist in Catholic Christianity, where it is maintained that the strictly contemplative life is justifiable for a limited number of persons who have the vocation for it. And here it must be added that even the Catholic contemplative is not exempt from one kind of world-transforming activity, that of intercessory prayer, for the existence of which there is no evidence among Hindu *yogis*. It would seem that Catholic contemplative activity also includes as an indispensable element a penitential section, comprising self-criticism, or self-examination, confession, and acts of will to amend. Further, some Catholic mystics, Tauler for instance, though deeply concerned with meditation and even ecstasy, found themselves impelled by their union with the glorified Christ to an intense social service of their suffering fellow-creatures.

Dr. Somervell records that when some senior boys in a mission school were taken for a holiday, an hour was set aside in the early morning each day for prayer and devotion. After a few days, some of the boys asked that this might be extended, as the one hour was insufficient. In Britain such a request would have sounded priggish. In India it was probably not. The other side of the picture is given by a man like Tyndale-Biscoe of Srinagar, who always stresses the weakness of the Indian temperament in the matter of truthfulness, unselfish and practical social service, and moral courage. He would contend that these things come less easily to those with the Hindu background and tradition than does *yoga*, and the evidence he gives seems to support his contention.

While Indian religion, even in its highest and most refined form, must seem to sympathetic Western observers weak in its world-transforming and welfare activities, it does not follow that it could not acquire greater strength in these directions without losing its specific features. Its adherents exhibit great potentialities for self-sacrifice, great responsiveness to the appeal of love, and great capacity for demonstrating the power of non-violence. The familiar saying 'the West needs the sound of a temple bell, but the East a clarion call', is not quite as true as it was, but insistence upon the universal necessity of developing the interior life is still India's strongest contribution to the sum-total of the world's religion, and it may well have been this that was the implication of the phrase with which this book opened: 'the efficiency of spirituality'.

It must not be imagined that the average Hindu is not just as much concerned as any Anglo-Saxon with food and wages. The point is that whereas the Anglo-Saxon ideals may be summed up as those of (i) success in business; (ii) social service; (iii) the winning of some trophy of heroism such as the Victoria Cross or the George Medal, the Hindu ideal is that of complete detachment from worldly interests, so that even social service is wholly detached and even performed with indifference as to its consequences. Neither the average Westerner nor the average Hindu may be ready to pursue these respective ideals himself. He will only too readily take the lower road. But he admires, when he sees them, those who have chosen the higher path and the narrower way.

I am not concerned in my capacity as a scientific observer with the appraisement of the relative qualities of Christianity and Hinduism. Were I to digress into such an investigation I should be exceeding my terms of reference. I would point out, however, that it is a matter for speculation whether those Indians are right in their conjecture who think that though unreformed Hinduism is probably inferior to the best forms of Christianity, it would, and could be, if reformed, similar to the best quality of Catholicism. In my judgment it would always remain different, on account of its low valuation of the time-process, and its uncertainty as to the relation of Deity to ethical values. But to say it would always be different is not the same as saying whether it would be superior or inferior to Christianity. On this matter I have my own convictions, which I will not intrude here.

A Note on Cow-Protection:

The attachment of sanctity to horned domestic cattle is found in many parts of the world, and is obviously connected with questions of food-supply, and with the attainment of a pastoral state by the particular people in question. Thus, the sacred dairy customs of the Bunyoro in central Africa have their analogy in the rather degraded and obviously declining milk ceremonies among the Todas of the Nilgiri Hills in India. Horned cattle were apparently treated with reverence in the days of the proto-Dravidian civilisation, if we may judge from the seals discovered by Sir John Marshall during the course of his investigations. The sacrifice of cattle is anathema to the orthodox Hindu, and although it is referred to in the *Taittiriya Brahmana*, it was apparently repugnant to the Dravidian element in the population, and only practised by the upper classes, among whom it gradually died out. The curious reverence for the cow and the sanctity accorded to the Saivite Brahminy bull in modern India is therefore of very ancient origin. It is a special case of a general attitude towards non-human organic life which prevails in India, and which is well expressed in the words of the Brihadaranyaka Upanishad:

'The Atman in Man is the very same as the vital force in the elephant, the gnat, the ant, the four quarters of the world; in short, the Atman in Man is part and parcel of the whole Universe.'

Yet, as it prevails today, it seems to observers an extravagance. A modern writer, Sundara Rama, quotes Monier-Williams with evident approbation as describing 'the superb attitude of Hindus towards the cow'. Monier-Williams says:

'The cow is of all animals the most sacred. Every part of its body is inhabited by some deity or other. Every hair on its body is inviolable. All its excreta are hallowed. Not a particle ought to be thrown away as impure. On the contrary, the water it ejects ought to be preserved as the best of holy waters—a sin-destroying liquid which sanctifies everything it touches, while nothing purifies like cow-dung. Any spot which a cow has condescended to honour with the sacred deposit of her excrement is for ever afterwards consecrated gound, and the filthiest place plastered with it is at once cleansed and freed from pollution, while the ashes produced by burning this hallowed substance are of such a holy nature that they not only make clean all material things, however previously unclean, but have only to be sprinkled over a sinner to convert him into a saint.'

Mr. Gandhi, writing in *Young India*, 1931, made the following remarks:

'Cow-protection is an article of faith in India. Apart from its religious sanctity it is an ennobling creed.

'Cow-protection is the dearest possession of the Hindu heart. It is the one concrete belief common to all Hindus. No one who does not believe in cow-protection can possibly be a Hindu.

'That which distinguishes Hinduism from every other religion is its cow-protection. The cow question is a big question, the greatest for a Hindu. Hindus do not fulfil their trust so long as they do not possess the ability to protect the cow.

'Cow-protection is one of the most wonderful phenomena in human evolution.

'Cow-protection is the gift of Hinduism to the world.'

Several more similar passages could be quoted from the same book. It is difficult to know how far to treat such remarks seriously. One learned Hindu to whom I submitted them replied that there was no cow-protection in the Vedas, and that Mr. Gandhi, though a pious man, was not a theologian. Yet it is impossible not to recognise that for popular Hinduism what he says is largely true, and that it is just this fanatical defence of the cow which often leads to conflict between Hindus and Moslems. Small wonder that some Indians with a modern education are beginning to murmur: 'A plague on both your houses.'

The difference between Indian and Western ways of regarding man's relation to the animal world is nowhere better illustrated than in one of the stories of the Pancharatra, where a king called Sivi is asked to arbitrate between a falcon and a dove. The king offers the falcon some dead meat if he will spare the dove, and the falcon replies: 'No, it is my nature to require live meat. If you deprive me of my natural prey, the living dove, you ought in justice to give me a proper alternative.' Thereupon the king declares that he will give the weight of the dove in his own flesh to the falcon. But when he proceeds to cut off pieces of his own flesh and to throw them in the scales they are not found heavy enough, whereupon the king leaps with his whole body into the pan. At the sight of such heroism and self-sacrifice the heavens open and two deities—Indra and Yama—descend to earth and exclaim: 'Well done, O King. We have realised your burning love for animals. You alone have known the real truth. Your body will again be whole and unhurt as before. May your inexhaustible wealth be always spent in acts of virtue benefiting all created beings.'

BOOKS FOR FURTHER STUDY

E. O. MARTIN. *The Gods of India.* Dent. 1914.

MRS. SINCLAIR STEVENSON. *The Rites of the Twice-Born.* Oxford. 1920.

C. E. O'MALLEY. *Popular Hinduism.* Cambridge. 1935.

J. MACKENZIE. *Hindu Ethics.* Oxford. 1922.

MISS AELFRIDA TILLYARD. *Spiritual Exercises* (esp. chapters ii, iii, and vi). S.P.C.K. 1927.

PROFESSOR S. N. DASGUPTA. *The Religion and Philosophy of Yoga.* Trübner's Oriental Series.

See also *Hinduism, the Source of its Power,* by RAJENDRA CHANDRA DAS, in *The International Review of Missions,* vol. xxix, No. 144.

10

SELF-GOVERNMENT AND
THE FUTURE OF HINDUISM

This chapter is actually being written at a time when a most momentous step has been taken by the British Raj. In the setting up of an Indian provisional government with the task entrusted to it of framing a constitution, and by the announcement that British administration in India is being placed definitely in the hands of her own people. It is, therefore, almost impossible to be sure of saying anything which might not prove to be out-of-date by the time it appeared in print. Only a few general observations on the broadest possible lines can wisely be ventured.

The influence of the reforming Hindus who were described in the eighth chapter has extended far outside their immediate circle of disciples, and although it has not yet reached the illiterate masses, it has provided educated Indians who had become discontented with orthodox and traditional Hinduism with some alternative to abandoning the latter for another faith. Thus, it is said that since the advent of neo-Hinduism there have been, as a consequence of it, fewer high-caste conversions to Christianity.

And further. The great growth of nationalism in India during the early twentieth century has made loyalty to Hinduism almost an essential part of the duty of a good Indian. Gandhi and Nehru have been mainly politicians, but Gandhi, on one side of his character, was a prophet who believed he had a message for humanity, and who acknowledged his indebtedness to Christ as well as Hindu tradition, though he remained an avowed Hindu. While, as a Hindu reformer, he stood for the very highest principles in the political struggle, sublimating the

Indian ethical ideal of *ahimsa* or harmlessness, rendering it positive by interpreting it as compassion, and making it the central feature of his programme, attacking caste, and introducing a new pacifist technique into demands for revolutionary political changes, yet he expressed great leniency towards popular Hinduism. Thus he wrote once:

'I know the vice that is going on today in all the great Hindu shrines, but I love them in spite of their unspeakable failings.'

'Cow-protection is the dearest possession of the Hindu heart. It is the one concrete belief common to all Hindus.'

'I do not disbelieve in idol-worship. . . . An idol does not excite any feeling of veneration in me. But I think that idol-worship is part of human nature. I do not consider idol-worship a sin.'[1]

Nehru, on the other hand, is an extremely honest agnostic, and is ready to liquidate a good many of the religious practices of his fellow-countrymen. Thus in 1928 he wrote: 'Our religion is one of the butcher, of what to touch and what not to touch, of baths and topknots, of all manner of marks and fasts and ceremonies that have lost all meaning. Our very gods are manufactured in the workshops of England or Japan,'[2] and again in 1944:[3] 'India must lessen her religiosity, and turn to science. She must get rid of the exclusiveness in thought and social habit which has become like a prison to her, stunting her spirit and preventing growth. The idea of ceremonial purity has erected barriers against social intercourse, and has narrowed the sphere of social action. The day-to-day religion of the orthodox Hindu is more concerned with what to eat and what not to eat, who to eat with and from whom to keep away, than with spiritual values. . . . Some Hindus talk of going back to the Vedas. . . . Idle fancies, for there is no going back to the past; there is no turning back, even if this were thought desirable. There is only one-way traffic in Time.'

Such being the opinions of the man who for this generation is one of the chief leaders in the setting up of the new Constitution, and who has already moved successfully a resolution for a sovereign independent republic of India, it is natural to ask, what are the prospects of Hinduism under the impending conditions?

To attempt anything like a complete answer would not only be difficult, but might easily involve one in rash and premature statements.

1 Quoted from *Young India* and from a work by C. F. Andrews entitled *Mahatma Gandhi's Ideas*, p. 40. *Young India* was written by Gandhi in 1930.
2 In *The New Era*. October 1928, p. 22.
3 In *The Discovery of India*, p. 447.

Probably the 1938 ten-year programme of the National Planning Committee[4] has the most direct bearing upon our problem, and since it has been published, it can safely be referred to. At first sight it seems to be mainly concerned with the social and physical well-being of the population, and it outlines five main points:

  (a) a balanced diet, with 2,400 to 2,800 calories for the adult worker;
  (b) provision of medical aid on the basis of one unit per 1,000 of the population;
  (c) improvement in clothing by a 100 per cent increase in the allowance of material *per capita* per annum;
  (d) housing standards to reach at least 100 square feet per individual;
  (e) an increase in the average expectation of life.

It is obvious that the radical alteration which is here the target, so far as the habits and material condition of the people are concerned, is bound to have a profound corresponding effect on their attitude to earthly existence. Will 'world-and-life-negation' under such altered conditions make its old appeal?[5]

But further. There is the avowed intention of the new government, when it gets into the saddle, of giving literacy to 165 millions of adult Indians in fifteen years. All this is in obvious imitation of the policy of the USSR, but what kind of result is it going to have upon the old popular Hinduism of the masses such as O'Malley described a few years ago? Even allowing for lapses into illiteracy, the total result is bound to be appreciable, though some doubt the capacity of Indians to administer their country well enough to make a ten-year plan effective.

Another item to be taken into consideration is the steady growth of Communist propaganda. Marxism in relation to religion has no more sympathy with higher Hinduism than with Christianity, and in the Asiatic territories of Russia it has done its best to dethrone Islam and Buddhism from the dominant position which they formerly held in

4 *See* Nehru, op. cit. pp. 336 ff.
5 The point may also well be made that during the British occupation of India, the military defence of the country and the preservation of order between discordant communities largely depended upon the presence of a foreign garrison, and this left the inhabitants themselves free to pursue spiritual and pacific ends without distraction. But in a self-governing India this comparative immunity from violence will disappear, and power may easily pass to those who possess military strength. Under such conditions world- and life-negation may be affected both by the necessity for maintaining a larger national army, and in some areas by the power being in the hands of those who are not well disposed to the presence of large bodies of ascetic recluses.

Bokhara and in Mongolia. It is plain therefore that any landslide in India in the direction of Marxism would mean a religious disintegration at least as great as that which occurred in the Russia of 1918;[6] and a noted anthropologist some time ago remarked to me upon the uncanny feeling he had of the resemblance between the life of the people in India and in pre-revolution Russia. In 1942 Congress wholeheartedly approved of the existence of the Communist Party of India, but three years later it was criticising its members as traitors. The reason for this change is that the CPI felt that it must, in a semi-feudal and semi-colonial country like India, work first for a bourgeois-democratic revolution, and the establishment of a new Indian democracy, and only in the second place for a socialist revolution and state, and Congress has felt (rightly or wrongly) that after the entry of the USSR into the war, the nationalist spirit in the CPI broke down. This has involved a set-back in the position of the CPI. At the same time the famine and misery which have ensued at the end of the war, and also the recent great growth of industrialism, with the fear of exploitation of the proletariat by Indian capitalists, and also the sense that in China, Burma and Malaya Communism is a growing force—all these may easily bring about a revival of the prestige of the CPI, and therefore Nehru's condemnation of it can only be regarded as a temporary set-back. Even the interim government has agreed to open diplomatic relations with the USSR and to exchange ambassadors. Yet in an independent India it may be a long time before the political programme of the CPI secures a working majority, and as long as Gandhi's influence lives, it seems more likely that the religious policy of the farmers and workers of any new constitution will continue along the lines indicated by Nehru in his book which he wrote in prison:[7]

'India must break with much of her past, and not allow it to dominate the present. Our lives are encumbered with the dead wood of this past; all that is dead and has served its purpose has to go. But that does not mean a break with, or a forgetting of the past. We can never forget the ideals that have moved our race, the dreams of the Indian people through the ages, the wisdom of the ancients, the buoyant energy and love of life and nature of our forefathers, their spirit of curiosity and mental adventure, the

6 Professor Hutton reports that in Bombay in recent years there has been formed an Anti-Priestcraft Association the purpose of which is stated to be 'to combat all religious and social beliefs and customs and institutions which cannot stand the test of reason', and members of which are reported to entertain a frankly bolshevist attitude towards all religions and to advocate the destruction of all temples, churches, and mosques. (Hutton, op. cit. p. 205.)

7 *The Discovery of India*, chapter x, p. 438.

K

daring of their thought, their splendid achievements in literature, art and culture, their love of truth and beauty and freedom, the basic value that they set up, their understanding of life's mysterious ways, their toleration of other ways than theirs, their capacity to absorb other peoples and their cultural accomplishments, to synthesise them, and develop a varied and mixed culture. Nor can we forget the myriad experiences which have built up our ancient race, and lie embedded in our sub-conscious minds. We will never forget them or cease to take pride in that noble heritage of ours. If India forgets them she will no longer remain India, and much that has made her our joy and pride will cease to be.

'It is not this that we have to break with, but all the dust and dirt of ages that have covered her up and hidden her inner beauty and significance, the excrescences and abortions that have twisted and petrified her spirit, set it in rigid frames, and stunted her growth. We have to cut away these ex-crescences and remember afresh the core of that ancient wisdom and adapt it to our present circumstances. . . . Old as we are, with memories stretching back to the early dreams of human history and endeavour, we have to grow young again, in tune with our present time, with the irrepressible spirit and joy of youth in the present and its faith in the future.

'Truth, as ultimate reality, if such there is, must be eternal, imperishable, unchanging. But that infinite, eternal and unchanging truth cannot be apprehended in its fullness by the finite mind of man, which can only grasp, at most, some small aspect of it limited by time and space, and by the state of development of that mind and the prevailing ideology of the period. . . . If some one aspect of the truth has been petrified by dogma in a past age, it ceases to grow and develop and adapt itself to the changing needs of humanity; other aspects of it remain hidden, and it fails to answer the urgent questions of a succeeding age. . . . Indeed, it is probably not even understood to the extent that it was understood in that past age when it grew up and was clothed in the language and symbols of that age. . . . Moreover, as Aurobindo Ghose has pointed out, every truth, however true in itself, yet, taken apart from others which at once limit and complete it, becomes a snare to bind the intellect, and a misleading dogma; for in reality each is one thread of a complete weft, and no thread must be taken apart from the weft.'

These are the words of one who is himself a liberal Brahmin. We set beside them the words of a liberal-minded Scot,[8] who, in describing Radakrishnan and Vivekananda as seeking to re-interpret Hinduism in a sense that will make moral struggle and effort a reality, remarks: 'to accomplish this, the whole system requires transformation', and

8 Dr. Nicol MacNicol: it is the recurrent theme in his Wilde Lectures delivered at Oxford in 1935.

again: 'unless Hinduism is splendidly untrue to itself . . . its world will remain to the end unredeemed'.

BOOKS FOR FURTHER STUDY

C. F. ANDREWS. (1) *The Real India.* (2) *Mahatma Gandhi's Ideas.*

PANDIT NEHRU. Op. cit., final chapter.

NICOL MACNICOL. Wilde Lectures. 1935.

NOTE TO 1962 EDITION

This book was written sixteen years ago, just before India gained her independence. My Indian friends tell me that there is nothing in its account of the past history of their religion which calls for alteration, and for this I am glad, although I know that I owe the fact very largely to the careful scrutiny of my original MS by some of the persons mentioned in its preface.

But during the sixteen years interval I have had the privilege of making as many as four visits to the new republic, and on one occasion of staying there for nearly a year. It would seem therefore that there is a good case for composing a new preface, to be set side by side with the old one, in which something is said about the present religious situation, and the effect of independence upon it.

First of all, I should like to stress the danger and difficulty of making generalisations about so large an area. It is like talking about the state of religion in Europe. No one would suppose it to be identical in the Orkneys and in Portugal. But the variations in India are all the greater because there still exist districts in which primitive and unsophisticated systems of belief and practice, such as those of the hill-tribe of the Samantas in the Paderu area of Andhra state or the fishing-tribe of the Jalaris near Visaghapatnam on the Bay of Bengal, remain almost untouched either by Christian missions, the acids of modernity, or even indigenous philosophic Hinduism, or some sort of bhakti theism; while in the greater centres of education attention is being paid increasingly to the most modern aspects of Western thought. This rich variety makes the Republic of India perhaps the only one on the face of the planet in which it is possible for the student of religion to see every conceivable sort of belief and practice still alive. The range is terrific, and if one includes the various Christian communities, as well as the pockets of Muslims still remaining, which include some Indian Sufis, one can truthfully assert that India still remains the greatest and most interesting workshop of religion in the world.

But in the second place, it is clear that among the intelligentsia there has been since 1946 a steady landslide away from religion. During the struggle for independence it was patriotic for a student to be a professing Hindu. I do not think this is the case today. Those who know the colleges are apt to declare that the vast proportion of their members have a vacuum instead of a working religious faith. Some are avowed humanists; some are Marxists; but most of them are only thinking about how they can cram up enough to pass an examination, acquire a degree, and slip into some sort of fairly remunerative job: and nearly all keep on saying that India is a backward country and *must* get on! Most of the scientifically trained Indians I have met, especially the doctors of medicine, are lax even about keeping the food-laws of the orthodox social system. With the spread of literacy and the provision of village radio loudspeakers, this growth of secularism is likely to spread to the huge rural areas, with results which nobody can foresee: and all the time the Marxists are busy; and their great appeal is to the poor, whose patience, though still pathetic, is slowly wearing out.

In the third place, there is certainly a resurgence of Hinduism in some quarters, encouraged no doubt by some conservative political groups like the Mahasabha, but congenial to those who, rejoicing in national independence, like to feel that they have a right to hold on to their inherited religious institutions, which include a good deal of pageantry at festivals, do not make too great demands on morality, and are deeply rooted in tradition and in the subconscious levels of the Indian mind. One of the most striking features in Indian life is the persistent belief in astrology. Many educated Indians seem to live in two worlds. In one, they behave as cultured and sceptical agnostic humanists, well acquainted with the principles of modern science. In the other, they appear as people giving preference to Ayurvedic medicine, and resorting to brahmins who can draw horoscopes or tell them which days will be auspicious for getting married or setting out on a journey. But the oppressive social system known as caste is steadily breaking down, and with it a great deal of traditional Hinduism is toppling as well.

In the fourth place, there is undoubtedly a marked increase in American influence. It is not that Americans are specially popular, but they have a vast amount of money to spend on good causes, and they use much of it upon projects for the material and spiritual welfare of India. Probably more Indians go to the USA for higher education than to Europe nowadays, because scholarships and grants are available there. The consequence of this is that an increasing number of Indians copy American social customs, and tend to follow 'the American way of life'. Since the USA is a republic, and has never ruled India, this is less likely to cause offence than to adopt practices which are definitely 'British', though this does not mean that the British are not popular, for they certainly are. A hard struggle is going on between America and Russia for the soul of India, and it is by no means clear so far that America is winning it, or that her propaganda is more skilful and convincing than that of the USSR.

It is natural to enquire what are the prospects for the spread of the Christian movement. Here one must be frank. A great deal of missionary propaganda has been and still is of the conservative and often fundamentalist variety, and much of this is treated with contempt by educated Indians, who know that it has no future in the countries from which it comes, and do not see why it should be foisted upon their own. Hence they are increasingly reluctant to give facilities for the entry of missionaries belonging to free-lance agencies. To get a visa you must often be sponsored either by Rome or by the United Christian Council in India. The situation varies naturally from State to State. Nevertheless the Federal Government is far from being hostile. It tries to adhere conscientiously to the principle of religious neutrality which has been written into the constitution, and it fully appreciates the excellent work done by Christian schools, colleges, and hospitals. If there is a debate on 'conversions' in the Lok Sabha, the subject tends to get talked out without a division, with perhaps the comment on the part of a leading politician that if anyone chooses to change his (or her) religion, it is no one's business but his own.

The recent census will show, one feels, a marked growth in the number of persons recording themselves as Christians, but against this has to be set the great increase in the size of the population, in spite of government effort at family planning; and of course the major part of this 'population explosion' is among the poorest, most illiterate, and most backward and superstitious. Still, wherever one goes, one finds Christian activity, though it often looks foreign rather than indigenous, and the church-members sometimes have the appearance of being *déraciné*, although one knows signal instances where this is not so at all.

Future prospects are uncertain. The atmosphere of India is so friendly and even hospitable to religious movements, and so vulnerable to the appeal of the Christian saint who really does follow his Master, that the churches may easily enter upon a new phase, with a wide and deepening extension of their work, especially in the moulding of the social order; and conversions, now slowed down, may again increase. But if India should move suddenly along the same path as China—and that is by no means impossible—the story of that country might be repeated, with, of course, some variations due to differences in national temperament.

INDEX

A

Abbasid Empire, 97
Aboth, Pirke, 50
adharma, 64
advaita, 62, 91ff., 104
Afghanistan, 74, 98 f.
Africa, 20
Agni, god of fire, 31, 46
  hymn to, 29
agnihotra, 128
ahimsa, 65
Ahuramazda, 33
Aitareya, Up., 50
Akbar, Mughal, 106 f.
Alberuni, 87, 98
Alexander the Great, 60, 74
Allahabad, *mela* or fair at, 131, 133
Alwars, the twelve, 87
Amarnath, cave in Kashmir, 132
Ambala, district in Punjab, 21
America, 14, 19
  Indians in, 63
Ameshaspentas, 34
amicitia, 71
Amiel, Henri Frédéric, 67
Amitabha, 77
amity, 71
Amsa, 34

Andaman Islanders, 20
Andrews, C. F., 47, 107, 111 f., 119
  121, 143 n., 147
Angiras, 29
Angkor, 68
Anti-priestcraft Association, 145 n.
Apollo, 123
Arabia, 14
Aranyakas, 45
Aranyi, 21
Arjuna, 78, 80
Arya desha, 13
Arya Dharma, 14, 16
Aryaman, 34
Aryans (Aryas), 14, 23–4, 30, 31
Arya Samaj, 14, 117 f.
asamsakta, 136
asanas, 135
asceticism, 52, 88
ashrama, 55
ashramas, the four, 129
Asoka, 74
atta, 67
attadipa, 67
Aurignacians, 20
australoids, 20, 22
avatar, 70, 77, 86, 87, 100
Ayudah puja, festival of, 130
Ayyar, Mr. Jagadisar, 128

B

Badrinath, shrine of, 132
Baghdad, 97
Bahram Yasht, the, 77
Bai, Mira, 100
Baigas, 21
bairagi, 132
Balaki, 55
Bali, 68
Baluchistan, 22
Belvalkar, Professor, 48
Benares, 20, 103, 104, 123
Bernard, St. of Clairvaux, 94
Bernier, French traveller in 1665, 123
Bhaga, 34
bhagat, 128, 132
bhagava, 66
Bhagavadgita, the, 72, 78 ff.
bhajans, 101, 126
bhakti, 85 ff., 100 ff.
bhaktiyoga, 122
Bharata varsha, 14
Bhils, 21
Bible, quotations:
  Genesis i, 46
  2 Samuel, i, 18 (R.V.), 30
  Micah vi, 56
  Psalm li, 56
Bihar, 70
Birla, Seth Raja Baldeolas, 14
bodhisattvas, 69, 77
Boghaz Keui, names of gods in inscription at, 32
Brahman (Brahma), 38 f., 50, 51, 58, 59, 67, 123
Brahmanas, 27, 44, 47
brahmayajna, 128
Brahmins, caste of, 38–9, 44 (Brahmans)
Brahmo Samaj, 113
brahmodya, 45
Brihadaranyaka Up., 59, 71, 139
British, occupation of India by the, 109 ff.
buddha, 66
Buddhism, 49, 63, 66 ff., 92

Bunyoro, 138
Burkitt, Professor F. C., 116
but-parast, 84

C

Camboja, Empire of, 68
Carey, William, 110 f.
Carpenter, Joseph Estlin, 96, 100
Caste, 36 ff., 120
  marks, 40 ff.
Catholicism, 15
Census-report, Indian, 14, 21
Ceylon, 22
Chaitanya, 101 f.
Chanakya, 74
Chandogya Up., 58, 60
Chandragupta II, 75
Chartism, 111
Chatterji, Gadadar, 118. (*See* also Ramakrishna Parahamsa)
Chenchian, Mr. P., 115 n.
Chenchus, 21, 31
China, 27 n.
  altar of heaven in, 32
Chota Nagpur, 21
Chronicle, Anglo-Saxon, 73
colonisation, Indian, 36, 68
Communists, in India, 145
cow-protection, 138 ff.
Creation, hymns of, 46
Cremation, 31

D

Dadupanthis, 105
Daksa, 34
dakshina, 30
Danquah, African theological treatise by, 111 n.
Das, Rajendra Chandra, 141
Das, Ram, 101
Das, Tulsi, 77, 103 ff.
Dasgupta, Professor S. N., 12, 13 n., 58 n., 61, 72, 74 n., 96 n., 141

dasya, 101
Dasyus or Dasos, 23
Datt, Narendranath, 118
Davids, Mrs. Rhys, 72
Deccan, 75
Delhi, sack of, 73 n., 98
Deo, H.H. Prince Bhanj, 12, 73 n., 83
Descartes, 54
Deussen, 49
devadasis, 129
Dewali, festival of lights, 130
dhamma (see dharma)
dharma, 64, 72, 124 f.
Diogenes, 60
Dionysus, 87, 123
Dirghatamas, 45
Disease, epidemic, in India, 35
Dodds, Professor E. R., 43
Dravidian, people, 22, 24, 37, 56
    language, 21 n.
    idols, 84
    cattle-cult among early peoples, 138–9
Dubois, Abbé, 110 f., 121
Durga, 107
Dutt, Romesh, 83
dvaita, 93

E

Eagle, Solomon, 64
Eckhart, 51, 91, 137
Eddington, Sir Arthur, 54
Edgerton, Professor Franklin, 83
Eliot, Sir Charles, quoted or referred to: 17, 39, 44, 56 f., 77, 88, 89, 90, 107
Ethelreda, Saint, 36
Etruria, 23

F

fakir, 132
Farquhar, Dr. J. N., 112 n.
Fathers, Cappadocian, 56
Festivals in India, 130 f.
flamen, 39 n.

Fox, George, 133
Franciscans, 74
Fuller, Sir Bamfylde, 133
Furies, the, 88

G

Gandhi, Mahatma, 15, 36, 79, 87, 109
    on cow-protection, 139–40
    compared with Nehru, 142–3
Ganesa, 124
Ganges, 123
    source of, 19
Garbe, 79
Garhwal, 132
Garratt, G. T., 17
Gathas, the, 24 n.
Gautama, Siddhartha, 36, 66 ff.
gayatri, the, sacred mantra, 127
George V, H.M. King, 87
Ghose, Sri Aurobindo, 83, 85, 92, 114 f 121
Glastonbury, 129
Glover, Dr. T. R., 17
Gonds, 21
gopura(m), 129
Goressio, 110
gosain, 132
Greek inscription, Vaishnavite, 75
Greeks, in India and Bactria, 75, 84, 87
Grierson, Sir George, 104
Griswold, H. D., quoted, 33, 42
gurus, 126

H

Harappa, 21, 22
Hari, 101
hatha yoga, 135
Hecataeus, 59
Heiler, Friedrich, 29
Heimann, Dr. Betty, 14 n., 15 n., 67
Heliodorus, son of Dion, Greek worshipper of Vishnu, 75
Himalayas, 19 f.
Hindu, origin of name, 13

Holi, festival of, 130
homa, sacrifice, 127
hotar, 30
Hrishikesa, 80
Hume, Professor R. E., quoted 50,
    51, 52, 54, 60
Hutton, Professor J. H., referred to,
    22 n., 23 n., 37 n., 38, 42, 86,
    133 n., 145 n.
Huxley, Aldous, 131

I

Ibbetson, Sir Denzil, 133
Iconography, Hindu and Buddhist, 84
Ignatius, Bishop of Antioch, on the
    Incarnation, 78 n.
Iliad, the, 78
Incarnation, Indian and Hellenistic
    ideas of, compared, 77 f.
Indonesia, 20, 36
Indra, god, 29
    hymn of, 29 f.
Indus Valley, 21, 22
Inge, Dr. W. R., 67
Iran, 26, 33
Isa (or Iswara), 59, 76
Islam, in India, 97 ff.
Israel, religion of, 16
ista, 54
Iyer, Mr. V. Krishnaswami, 53

J

Jagannath, 87, 123
Jaidev, 106
Jains, Jainism, 14 n., 63 ff., 69
jàti, 37
Jina, 64
Jiva, 64
jñanayoga, 122
Jñanesvar, 94 f.
Judaism, 15, 69

K

Kabir, 100, 104 ff.
Kabirpanth, the, 105
Kadars, 20
Kafirs, red, 23 n.
Kailas, Mount, 19
Kali, goddess, 107
    temple of, 118
Kalidasa, the Gita quoted by, 78, 83
Kallar, the, as bullfighters, 22 n.
Kamadeva, 123
Kamakhya, 106
Kanishka, 75
Kapilavasthu, 66
karma, 52, 53
karmayoga, 122
Karna, 78
Katha, Up., 48, 49, 54, 58, 71
Kathiawar, 21, 75
Kaushitaki, Up., 71
Keith, Professor A. Berriedale, 42, 4
    61
Kena, Up., 58
Keshab Chunder Sen, 113, 118
Khusran, Amir, 99
kirtans, 101, 126
Krishna, 80, 86, 87, 123
Kshatriyas, 37, 53, 63, 64, 68, 70
    rivalry with Brahmins, 39
Kumarappa, Bharatan, 96
Kurral, the, 125
Kushans, 75

L

Lakshmi-Narayan, temple of, at New
    Delhi, 14, 129
Laver, Mr. James, 135
lebensraum, desire for, among proto-
    Nordics, 28, 34
libido, 52
lila, 90
lingam, the, 89 f., 126
Logos, the, 104
Lounsbery, Mr. G. C., 72

Luther, comparison with Gautama discussed, 72
    hymns of, 100

M

McAuliffe, Dr. M. A., 108
Mackay, E. J., 25
Mackenzie, J., 140
MacNicol, Dr. N., quoted: 29, 32–3, 83, 94, 96, 102, 108, 146, 147
madhurya, 101
Madhva, 93
Mahabharata, the, 76
Mahavira, 64
Mahayana, 68, 77
Mahmud of Ghazni, Sultan, 97
Malapantaram, 21
mana, 30
Manasa, 124
Mandukya, Up., 52, 58
mantras, 127
Manu, Laws of, 72
Mari Meri, 124
Mariamma, 123
Marks, distinguishing (sectarian), 40 ff.
Marsh, Professor F. S., 24 n.
Marshall, Sir John, 21, 139
Marshman, 110
Martel, Charles, 97
Martin, E. O., 140
Martyn, Henry, 110
Marxism, 34, 56, 111, 144–5
Matarisvan, 45
maths, 133
Maurya, Chandragupta, 74
    dynasty, 74
Mediterranean culture, 22 n.
Megasthenes, 123
Menander, 75
metta, 71
Milinda (*see* Menander), 75
Mimamsa, Purva, 62
    Sutra, 96
    Uttara, 62
Mithras, 17, 123

Mitra, 34, 45
Mohammed, 56, 97
Mohenjodaro, 21, 22
moksha, 52
Monasticism in India, 70, 91, 133
    in Egypt, 36
    in Europe, 35
    in Tibet, 36
Mongols, 75
moral treatises, Indian, 125
Mozoomdar, Pratap Chandra, 113
Mukerjee, Professor Radhakamal, 121
Mundaka, Up., 51, 54, 58
Munro, Sir Thomas, 110
Muttra, 87, 117

N

Nagas, 22
Naladiyar, the, 125
Nalayiram, the, 87
Namdev, 101
Nanak, 105
Naraniya, the, 78
Narayana (collector of Upanishads), 47
Narayana, Swami, 101
Natarajan, Mr., Editor of the *Indian Social Reformer*, 129
negation, world- and life-, 34
negritos, 20, 21
Nehru, Pandit Jawaharlal, 14, 16, 21 n., 35, 39, 56–7, 99, 109, 120, 121, 143, 144 n., 145, 147
Neill, Bishop Stephen, 90 n., 125 n.
Nerbudda, 123
Nestorians (Christians), 90, 104
Nidagha, 91–2
nirvana, 52
Nordics, 23–4, 37, 56
Nyaya, 62

O

Oldenburg 48
O'Malley, Mr. C. L., quoted, 132, 140, 144

Oraons, 21
Otto, Professor Rudolf, 79, 83, 88, 91–2, 96
Ouranos, 32

P

Pai, Mr. D. A., 41
Pallas Athene, 123
Pan, 87
Pancharatra, the, Story from, 140
Pandharpur, 95
Pandya, 98
Paradise, in Vedic religion, 31
Paramatman, 66
pariahs, 37
Parjanya, 34
Parsva, 64
Perron, Anquetil du, 47, 51
peyote, 63
pilgrimages, 131–2
Pippalada, 55
Pitri-puja, 31
Planning Committee, National, 36, 144
Plato, 60
Plotinus, 136
Plutarch, 119
Polytheism, 123
Pope, Dr., 89 n.
Portuguese, 'castus', use of, 37
pneuma, 56
Prabandhar, the, 87
prakrti, 62
Pralhada, 94
prana, 56
pranayama, 127 f.
pranpratishta, 126
Prarthana Samaj, 120
Prasna, Up., 58
Pratt, Professor J. B., 72
pratyahara, 135
Prem Sagar, the, 95
Process, Dialectic, 56
Prophets, Hebrew, 56
Prthivi, 32

Przyluski, 86, 89 n.
Przywara, 51
psuedo-Dionysius, 51, 83
puja, 89 n.
Puranas, 95, 112
Puri, 95
purohit(a), 30, 127
purushas, 62

R

Radegund, Saint, 36
Radhakrishnan, Sarvepalli, 83, 114 ff., 146
Radhaswamis, 105
Raghubasmani (epithet of a Vaishnavite *avatar*, applied to George V), 87
raja yoga, 135
Rajputana, desert of, 19
Ram Mohan Roy, Raja, 112 f.
Ram Tirath, Swami, 119
Rama, hero-king, 76, 77, 94
Rama, Sundara, 139
Ramanand, 100
Ramanuja, 91 ff.
Ramat, 100
Ramakrishna Mission, the, 119
Ramakrishna Parahamsa, 118
Ramayana, the, 76 ff., 103, 110, 127
Ramkrishna, 94
Ranade, Mr. Justice, 119 f.
Rawlinson, H. G., 17
Rawson, Dr. J. N., 48, 54, 61
Ribhu, 91,
Rig-Veda, the, 31, 32, 34, 45 f., 52
rita, 32
Ritualism in India, 44 f.
Roman history, 23
Russell, Lord, 54, 60 n.
Russia, south-east, 23

S

Sabha, the, 136
sacrifice, human, 106

sadhu, 60, 128, 132 f.
Sailendra, dynasty of, 68
Saivism, 86, 87 ff., 90
Sakalya, 56
sakhya, 101
Sakti, 88
Saktism, 106
Salagrama stone, 126
samadhi, 64
    perpetual, 137
    samprajnata and *asamprajnata*, 134
Sāmkhya, philosophy, 49, 62, 67
samsara, 52
Samyutta, the, quoted, 68
Sanatanists, 14
Sanatkunara, 55
sāndhya, daily ceremony, 127 f.
Sanga, the dynasty, 74
Sankara, 91 ff.
sannyasi, 128, 132
Sanskrit, 26, 43
santi, 101
Sarapis, 17
Sarasvati, 123
Sarasvati, Dayanand, 117
Sarunta, 21
Satnamis, 105
Sattrayana, 54
Satvapatti, 136
Scandinavians, 23
Schopenhauer, 68 n.
Schwartz, 110
Schweitzer, Albert, referred to, 34
    quoted, 111
Scythians, 75
Seleucus, 74
Self, the Great, 58, 67
Senussi, compared with Sikhs, 105
Shahab-ud-din Ghuri, 98
shamans, 63
Shastri, Professor, quoted, 27 n.
Shaw, Mr. George Bernard, 56
Shinto, monotheism developing in, 33
Shorter, Mr. A.W., 87 n.
Shukoh, Prince Dara, 47
sikhara, 129

Sikhs, 14, 105 f.
Sind, occupation of, by Moslems, 98
sisna-devah, 22
Sitala, 123 f.
Siva, 19, 22, 123
smriti, 84, 96
Snake-worship, 124
soma, 29, 30, 63
Somervell, Dr., 73 n., 122, 137
sraddha, 31
Sravana, month of, festival of goddess
    of smallpox in it, 130
Srinagar, burial-place of Sankara, 92
Sriperumbur, 92
sruti, 28, 85, 96
Stevenson, Mrs. Sinclair, 72, 128, 130,
    131 n., 140
subchechcha, 136
Sudras, 37
Suffolk, 'sele', 70 n.
Sumeria, civilisation of, 21, 27 n.
svadhyaya, 128
Svetasvatara, Up., 50
Syrians (Christians), 90 n.

T

Tacitus 73
Tagore, Rabindranath, 108, 109 f.,
    113 f., 120, 121
Taittiriya, Up., 58
Tambyah, Mr. Isaac, 90
Tantras, 95, 106
tāpās, 63
tathagata, 66
Temples, worship in, 128-9
Tengalais, 93
tephillim, 41
Theophrastus, 15
Thomas, Dr. E. J., quoted, 29, 79, 82,
    83
thread, investiture with sacred, 127
Thucydides, 73
Tibetans, use of barley by, 30
Tillyard, Miss Aelfrida, 135, 141

Timour, 98
Tirumurai, the, 89
Tiruvaçagam, the, 89
Titus, Dr. M. T., 108
Todas, 21, 138
tomamasana, 136
Torah, the Jewish, 125
Travancore, 21, 90
Trismegistos, Hermes, 55
tsitsith, 41
Tukaram, 94, 101 ff.
tulasi, plant, 126, 131
Tulsi Das, poet, 77
Tyndale-Biscoe, Canon, 137

U

Uddav, 94
Upanishads, 27, 43 ff., 63, 110
    lists of, 47-9
Uralis, 20
Ushas, 31

V

Vaçagar, Manikka-, 89 ff.
Vadagalais, 93
Vaishesika, 62
Vaishnavism, 76, 86 ff.
Vaisyas, 37
Valhalla, 32
Vallabha, 100-1
Valmiki, 76
vamsa, 50
Vardhamana, 64
varna, 24, 37
Varuna, 32 ff., 45
Vasudeva, 76
vatsakya, 101
Vedanta, the, 62, 91
Vedas, the, 26 ff., 125
Verethragna (Vrttahan), 77

vicharana, 136
vidya, 55
Vidyapati, 100
vihara, 70
Vijaya Dharma Suri, 66
Vijayanagar, 98 f.
Vindhya hills, 20
Virjanand, Swami, 117
vishistadvaita, 52, 93
Vishnu, 123 (*see also* Vaishnavism)
Vithoba (Vitthata), 86, 95
Vivekananda, Swami, 13 n., 119, 121,
    146
vows, 131 f.

W

Wesley, John, compared with San-
    kara, 91
Williams, M. Monier, 112, 121, 139
Wilson, Dr. John, 133
worship, Hindu, 126 ff.

Y

yajña, 54
Yajñavalkya, 49, 52, 55, 56, 72
Yama, 46
Yamuna-muni, 92
yoga, 55, 62, 132 ff.
    six types of, 134
yogi, 132
Yueh Chih, the, 75

Z

Zarathustra, 24 n.
Zen (Buddhism), 92
Zendavesta, 47
Zeus (Dyaus), 32, 123
Ziegenbalg, 110
Zoroastrianism, 106